CLOCKS

OTHER BOSTON CHILDREN'S MUSEUM ACTIVITY BOOKS BY BERNIE ZUBROWSKI:

Ball-Point Pens

Bubbles

Messing Around with Baking Chemistry

Messing Around with Drinking Straws

Messing Around with Water Pumps

Milk Carton Blocks

Raceways: Having Fun with Balls and Tracks

Wheels at Work: Building and Experimenting
  with Models of Machines

CLOCKS

Building and Experimenting with Model Timepieces

BY BERNIE ZUBROWSKI

ILLUSTRATED BY
ROY DOTY

A Boston Children's Museum
Activity Book

Morrow Junior Books / New York

Printed in the United States of America.
1   2   3   4   5   6   7   8   9   10
Library of Congress Cataloging-in-Publication Data
Zubrowski, Bernie.
Clocks.
(A Boston Children's Museum activity book)
Summary: Instructions for using readily available
materials to make working models of different kinds of
clocks with suggested experiments to discover how they
work.
1. Clocks and watches—Juvenile literature. [1. Clocks
and watches] I. Doty, Roy, 1922-   ill.   II. Title.
III. Series.
TS545.Z83   1988   681.1'13   87-18467
ISBN 0-688-06926-6 (lib. bdg.)
ISBN 0-688-06925-8 (pbk.)

CONTENTS

INTRODUCTION

Today we are practically surrounded by clocks. In our homes we may have a grandfather clock in the living room, a timer on the stove in the kitchen, and a clock radio in the bedroom. At your school there are clocks in every classroom. There are clocks in stores, banks, offices, and even cars. Outdoors there are large clocks near the tops of churches and tall buildings. If you look around in a room full of people, many of them will probably be wearing wristwatches. You may be wearing one yourself right now.

We depend on all these clocks to tell us when to go to school or work, when to catch a plane, or when to turn on our favorite television program. In our modern age, it is hard to imagine how we could live without them.

Yet not so very long ago, few people had clocks or watches. In the country, farmers woke up very early in the morning just before sunrise and went to bed after sunset. People in towns divided their days into segments, shopping and eating approximately the same time each day. This doesn't mean that there weren't any clocks around, rather that very few people had them, and the clocks in clock towers weren't very accurate.

Although accurate clocks are a relatively recent development, people have been fascinated with measuring time for thousands of years. The earliest timekeepers were very simple, based on the regular movements of the sun, moon, and planets. Some of the first clocks go back to the days of the early Egyptians, who measured the changing water level in a dripping clay pot. Later, mechanical clocks were the most precise and advanced machines of their time.

There have always been scientists and tinkerers trying to invent new and ingenious ways of measuring time. This book will show you how to follow in their footsteps by making models of different kinds of clocks. Some are quite simple to construct, while others will require lots of patience and perseverance. All of the models can be made from materials you can find around your house or at a nearby hardware store.

In addition to the challenge of building a model and getting it to work properly, you can have fun using it to do some basic experiments. Experimenting with your models will help you to understand better how clocks work. This will give you the opportunity to solve problems and make discoveries the way real scientists and engineers do. Along the way you will also learn about the history of timekeeping and how clocks have changed from the simple measuring of a shadow to the complicated timing devices of today.

THE FIRST CLOCKS

You are out walking in the woods or playing in a park. You are supposed to be home by a certain time, and you don't have a watch. Can you think of a way to figure out the approximate time of day?

People in ancient times had to invent a way to do this, and even today some farmers and others who work out-doors can tell when it is time to head home without using a watch. Their method is simple. They watch the changing shadows of trees, rocks, or, in some places, the shadows cast by hills or mountains. In the morning these objects cast shadows in one direction, while in the afternoon the shadows fall in a completely opposite direction. By keeping track of the length of these shadows and how they change, one can make a good guess at the time of day.

Just how accurate is this practice? You can make some observations to find out.

The Sundial

The earliest known way of timekeeping seems to have been based on the observation of natural shadows. Various devices were invented to make these observations more accurate and consistent. These devices were called *sundials*. Although there are no remains of the earliest ones, there is evidence that sundials were used by the Babylonians more than 2,000 years ago. Some of the large monuments in Egypt, such as the pyramids, may have been used as sundials. The early Romans and Arabs made small sundials like those shown here.

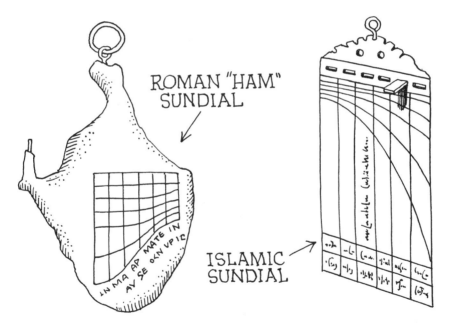

ROMAN "HAM" SUNDIAL

ISLAMIC SUNDIAL

Sometimes the shadow of a person would be used. Meetings were planned for a time when a person's shadow was a certain number of times the length of his or her own foot.

The Arabs made a hand-held sundial called the *astro-labe*, which they continued to use for several hundred years.

ARABIC
ASTROLABE

Sundials were still in use as recently as a hundred years ago, and some people use larger versions of them as decorations in their gardens even today.

You can find out for yourself how a sundial works just by carrying out some systematic observations. All you need is a marking device, such as chalk or masking tape, and pencil and paper to keep track of your observations.

Find a vertical pole or signpost outside your house or school that is in sunlight most of the day. Or look for a building whose shadow you can see for most of the day. You may even have a window in your house or classroom facing south, which lets in sunlight for a good portion of the day. You can then watch the shadows of the window frames as they move across the floor or a wall.

Start watching early in the morning. Make a mark on the ground with the piece of chalk, or place a piece of masking tape on the floor along the length of the shadow. When you first do this, stay for a while, watching how the shadow changes in relation to the mark you have just made. You may be surprised at how quickly the shadow moves off this mark. Come back every hour or two and continue to mark where the shadow is and its length. Keep a record of where the shadows fall and how their length changes.

Here is a record of a shadow during one day in the month of June.

While recording your observations over a period of days or weeks, here are some questions to consider:

How much does the shadow move in one hour?
When are the shadows the longest?
When are they the shortest?
Do the shadows fall at exactly the same spots from day to day or week to week?

To be able to answer the last question more precisely, you can make a small sundial.

You will need:
    1 broomstick or other small stick, 8 inches long
    1 flat piece of wood, about 2 feet square
    several pieces of paper the same size as the wood
    hammer
    nails
    masking tape
    pen or pencil

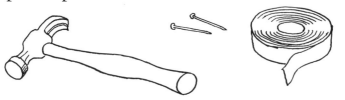

Step 1. Nail the stick to the flat piece of wood as shown on page 13.
Step 2. Tape a piece of paper on the flat surface of the wood.
Step 3. Locate a flat place where you can put this board without it being disturbed. Make a permanent mark on the ground, outlining the board. This way you can place your sundial in the same spot each day.

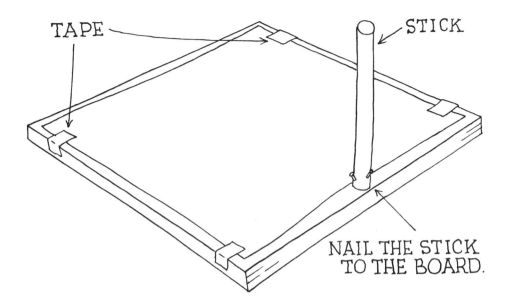

TAPE

STICK

NAIL THE STICK
TO THE BOARD.

EXPERIMENTS TO TRY

Draw a line on the paper to show how long the shadow is at different times of the day. Make a note of the times and date. Save the paper at the end of the day.

Try to record several daily observations at the same times each day. Do this over a period of several weeks. Better still, keep track of your observations over a period of several months. Make sure to use a new sheet of paper for each day.

WHAT'S HAPPENING?

As you have seen, the shadow of an object is continually moving. The shadow starts out long in the morning, becomes shorter as midday approaches, and lengthens again in late afternoon. This happens because the sun is near the horizon in the morning and late afternoon. At midday the sun is almost directly overhead.

The shadow is the shortest at midday. Depending on the time of year and where you are on earth, midday will sometimes be the same as twelve o'clock noon. You can find out exactly when midday occurs by consulting your local newspaper. The weather section will also print the times of sunrise and sunset. By counting up the total number of hours between sunrise and sunset and dividing by two, you can determine exactly when the sun is midway through its travels for that day.

If you have kept long-running records of the shadows cast by sticks and other structures, you should see that their length changes during the course of a year. In winter the shadows are longer, whereas they become shorter during the summertime.

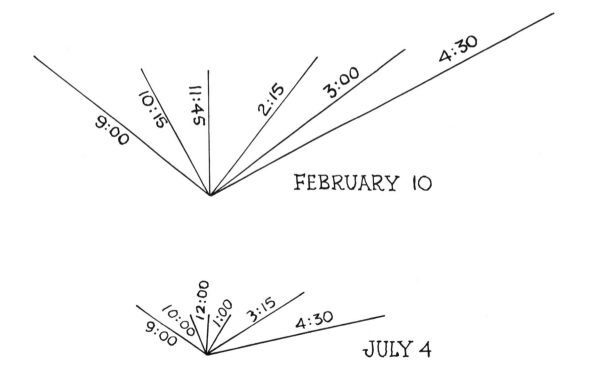

To understand why this happens, you have to imagine being on a spaceship far away from the earth, where you can see both the earth and the sun. You can create a small model of this. Find a large ball such as a volleyball or basketball. Put a toothpick or matchstick on the ball, holding it upright in place with some clay or gum. Place a lamp without a shade in the middle of the room (the lower the wattage of the bulb, the better the result). Position yourself a few feet from the lamp and hold the ball so that the toothpick casts a short shadow on the ball.

The ball represents the earth, and the toothpick is your sundial. Stand in one place and rotate the ball so that part of the time the toothpick casts a shadow and part of the time it is in the dark. This is similar to the daily rotation of the earth on its axis.

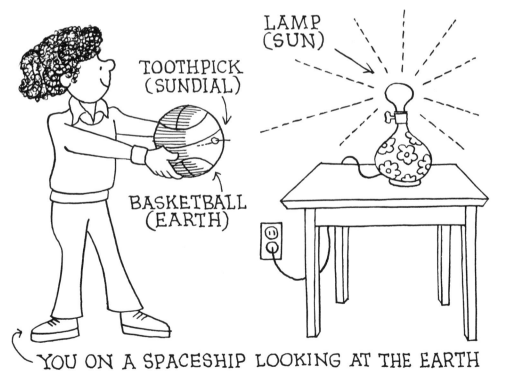

TOOTHPICK
(SUNDIAL)

LAMP
(SUN)

BASKETBALL
(EARTH)

YOU ON A SPACESHIP LOOKING AT THE EARTH

A Moon Position-Finder

The ultimate clock is the sun. All other clocks are based on its movements. But the passage of time may also be marked by careful observation of other heavenly bodies.

Ancient peoples were close observers of the heavens. They noticed that the movement of the moon and the stars was very orderly and formed repeating patterns. Farmers of long ago determined when they should plant in the spring by keeping track of the position of the sun in the sky and the number of full moons since they last planted. Certain yearly ceremonies were also determined by the number of full moons between one event and another.

It took thousands of years, however, before these patterns were fully understood. It wasn't until scientists such as Copernicus, Kepler, and Newton devised special mathematical formulas that accurate predictions of the movements of the stars and the moon could be made.

You can make some simple discoveries on your own. All you have to do is observe the moon and the stars on a regular basis and record your observations. You don't have to do this every night, but it is important to do it at the same time each night and over a long-enough period of time so that you can begin to recognize some kind of pattern.

Once you locate the moon in the sky, it is helpful to determine its position in relation to nearby trees or buildings. Then you can determine how quickly it is moving across the sky and can compare its location from one night to the next.

To make a moon position-finder, you will need:

    1 package of index cards, 5 inches by 8 inches
    1 drinking straw
    1 pin
    1 small nail or washer
    1 piece of string, 6 inches long
    masking tape
    pen or pencil

Step 1. Tape the drinking straw to one long edge of an index card.

Step 2. Tie a pin to one end of the string and the washer or nail to the other end.

Step 3. Place the pin in the center of the card, just under the straw.

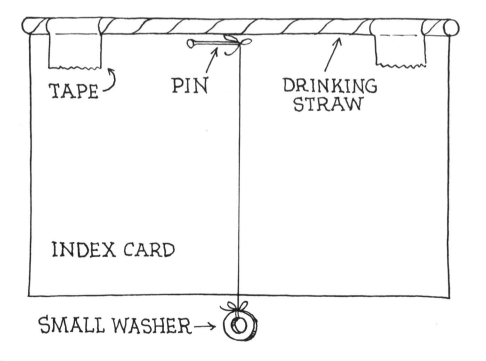

TAPE   PIN   DRINKING STRAW

INDEX CARD

SMALL WASHER →

EXPERIMENTS TO TRY

Hold the drinking straw up to your eye and line up the moon so that you can see it through the straw.

MAKE A MARK WITH A PEN WHERE THE STRING HANGS.

MOON

Draw a line on the card where the string is hanging. Write the date and time on the card. The position of the string line indicates whether the moon was sighted near the horizon or very high in the sky.

MOON LOW IN SKY

JULY 4
9:30

MOON HIGH IN SKY

AUGUST 8
9:30

Use another card to make a rough drawing of where the moon is, relative to some trees and buildings at the time of your observation.

Remove the straw and string from the first card, and save these two cards together for your records.

Use the string and straw again on new cards for further observations.

To help plan your observation dates and times, you may want to think about the following questions:

Can you find the moon in the sky at any time during the day?

Is the moon always in the same position in the sky at the same time each day or night? If not, how does this position change daily?

Can you always see the moon right after the sun sets?

Does the moon seem to move across the sky at the same rate as the sun?

How many days are there between one full moon and another?

How many days are there between a full moon and no moon?

Do full moons always happen on the same day of the month?

WHAT'S HAPPENING?

As you can see from your observations, the part of the moon visible to the earth goes through a regular series of changes. From one full moon to another, it appears to shrink in size until it reaches a point where there is almost no moon at all. Then it gradually appears larger and larger every day, until it is full again.

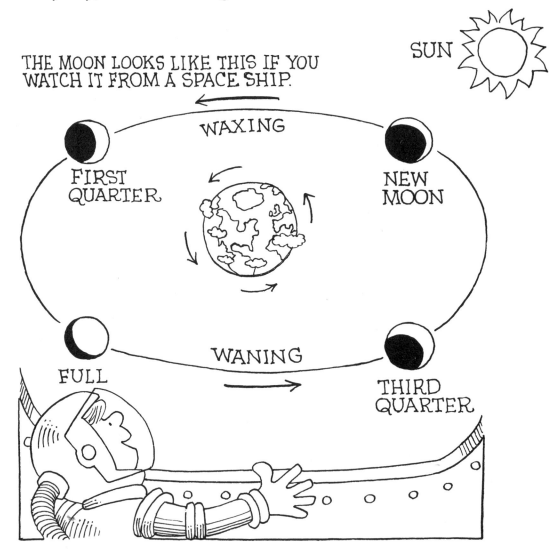

THE MOON LOOKS LIKE THIS IF YOU WATCH IT FROM A SPACE SHIP.

SUN

WAXING

FIRST QUARTER

NEW MOON

FULL

WANING

THIRD QUARTER

These changes are called *phases*, and they take place over a period of twenty-nine to thirty days. The full moon doesn't appear on the same day every month. In fact, there can be two full moons in a month, as shown on the calendar.

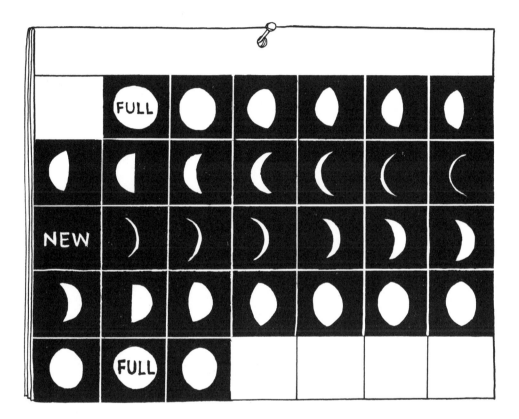

The moon can sometimes be seen during the day. If you have made careful observations of sunsets and moon rises, you will have noticed that each night following a full moon the moon appears on the horizon later and later, until it continues to be visible in the daytime. One or two days and nights each month you will barely be able to see the moon at all. This phase is called the *new moon*.

WATER CLOCKS

While washing dishes, hanging around at the beach, or helping your baby brother or sister take a bath, you have probably played with containers and water. You may have had fun just pouring water from one container into another or letting it drip out through holes while watching the water level inside the container change quickly or slowly. You probably never thought that what you were doing was useful or important. Yet for thousands of years people tried to discover ways to control the flow of water from one container to another in order to measure the passage of time.

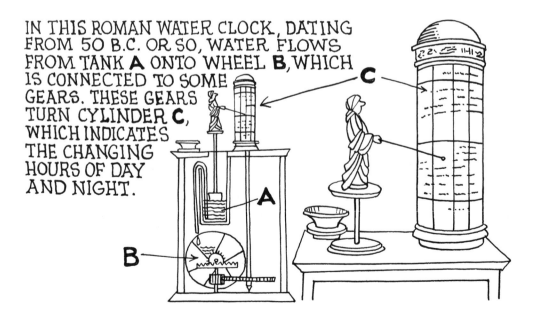

IN THIS ROMAN WATER CLOCK, DATING FROM 50 B.C. OR SO, WATER FLOWS FROM TANK **A** ONTO WHEEL **B**, WHICH IS CONNECTED TO SOME GEARS. THESE GEARS TURN CYLINDER **C**, WHICH INDICATES THE CHANGING HOURS OF DAY AND NIGHT.

Water clocks are among the oldest and simplest kinds of timekeepers. Some were in use in a part of the world called Babylonia as far back as the sixteenth century B.C. The Egyptians, Greeks, Indians, and Arabs either invented their own water clocks or copied devices from other peoples—all the while attempting to improve their accuracy.

In this chapter, you will learn how to construct some simple model water clocks from ordinary materials and to carry out some basic experiments. In this way you can face the same challenges and try to overcome the same types of problems that the ancients encountered.

Simple Water Clocks

To get started making the simplest type of water clock, gather together a large number of containers of different sizes and shapes. Try to find tin cans, paper cups, plastic tumblers and bowls, margarine and cottage-cheese tubs, milk cartons of different sizes, and plastic soda bottles of 1-, 2-, and 3-liter capacity.

Using the materials listed below, try different ways of having water flow out of the containers you have collected.

You will need:
>
>several nails of different sizes
>hammer
>straight pins
>measuring cup
>empty ball-point pen tubes
>oil-base modeling clay

several buckets
wall clock, alarm clock, or watch
pencil
paper

EXPERIMENTS TO TRY

The following experiments include the brief steps necessary to make your models and some questions to consider while you are working. Be sure to have a clock or watch nearby to check the timing of your constructions. You will also find it helpful if you keep a written record of your results as you go along. Remember, experimenting with water can get messy, so have plenty of towels as well as some buckets or a sink or tub nearby. This way you can clean up any spills and will also be able to recycle the water.

Punch a pinhole in the bottom of a container. Then punch a nail hole in the bottom of another container of the same type. Temporarily blocking the holes with some modeling clay, fill each container with water. Is there a big difference in the time it takes to empty the two containers?

Line up a set of nails according to thickness. Starting with the thinnest, punch a hole in the bottom of a container and then time how long it takes to empty the container completely. Push the next largest nail through the same hole and repeat the filling, emptying, and timing procedures. Continue to repeat these operations until you have used the thickest nail. What is the difference in emptying time from one nail to the next?

Keeping the hole size the same and using the same amount of water each time (check this with a measuring cup), is there a difference in emptying time for containers of different sizes and shapes? *Note:* For containers with large openings, such as soda bottles, you can better control the flow of water by filling the mouth of the bottle with clay and inserting a ball-point pen tube through the clay.

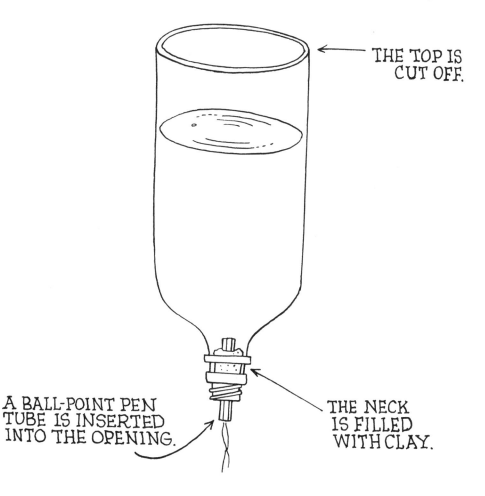

THE TOP IS CUT OFF.

A BALL-POINT PEN TUBE IS INSERTED INTO THE OPENING.

THE NECK IS FILLED WITH CLAY.

Judging by eye, does water flow out of a container at the same rate when the container is nearly full as compared to when it is almost empty?

Punch a hole in the bottom of a paper half-gallon milk carton. Punch a hole in the side of another carton. Fill both with water and record how long it takes each to empty.

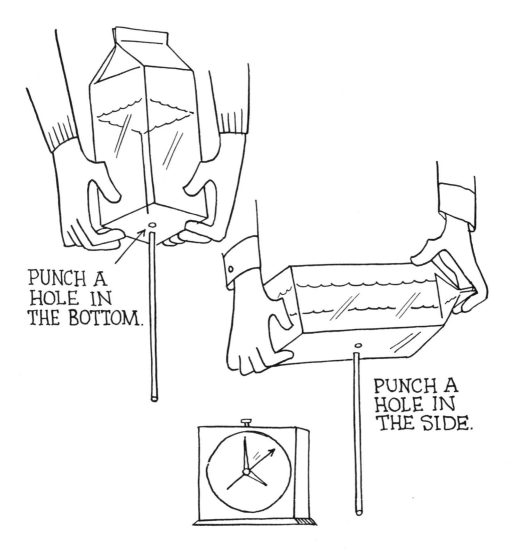

PUNCH A HOLE IN THE BOTTOM.

PUNCH A HOLE IN THE SIDE.

Repeat this activity with other pairs of containers. Keeping the hole size and the amount of water the same, does it matter where the hole is located in a container?

Using what you have learned from these activities, can you now make a water clock that goes for one minute from the time it first starts emptying until it is completely empty? Can you make a two-, three-, or five-minute water clock?

Using just one container, is there a way of indicating when one-, two-, three-, four-, or five-minute intervals have passed without starting over for each minute?

WHAT'S HAPPENING?

By now you should have discovered that you can make water clocks that measure from one to five minutes or more by carefully choosing the right combination of container and hole size. For instance, a 7-ounce paper cup with a nail hole made by a 2-inch-long nail in the bottom will take about one minute to empty. An hour clock would require a very small hole in a large container such as a 3-liter soda bottle.

This seems fairly simple, but if you have done your experiments carefully you should have noticed some curious results. For example, it took almost twice as long for the water to run out of the milk carton that was lying on its side as it did out of the carton with the hole in the bottom. This would indicate that it does matter where a hole is located in a container, even though you are using the same size hole and the same amount of water.

You may also have noticed that the water flowed much faster when a container was almost full as compared to when it was almost empty. To understand why this happens, you need to demonstrate to yourself how the weight of water pushes down on itself.

Fill two empty milk cartons with water, seal the tops securely, and try lifting both of them together. They can be very heavy. Then place these two cartons next to each other on your arm.

You can feel that the total weight on your arm is heavy, but each milk carton is only pressing down on one spot.

How does it feel if you stack the two milk cartons on top of each other?

You are holding up the same weight, but it is distributed differently. Now only one spot on your arm is supporting all the weight. Imagine twenty or thirty milk cartons stacked vertically on your arm. The weight would be unbearable!

Look again at the water in a tall container. Each inch of water is similar to the filled milk cartons on your arm. The more inches of water that are piled on top of each other, the greater the force at the bottom of the container. The greater the force, the faster the flow of water out of the container.

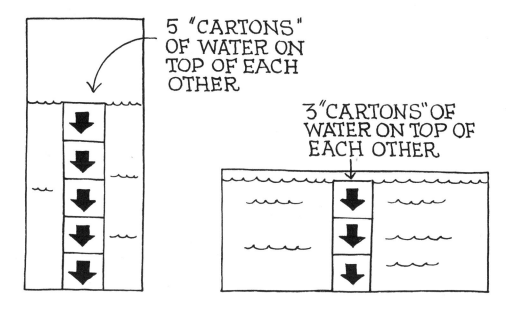

5 "CARTONS" OF WATER ON TOP OF EACH OTHER

3 "CARTONS" OF WATER ON TOP OF EACH OTHER

Also, as water is draining out of a container, there is less and less water pushing down on the opening at the bottom. This results in a slower rate of flow toward the end of the draining process as compared to the beginning. This creates a problem when you want to make a clock which indicates one-minute intervals. You cannot simply measure off equal lengths on the side of the container and assume that the water flows out so many inches every minute.

There are ways of overcoming this problem, however, and the next sections will show you several techniques devised by the ancients.

The Chinese Water Clock

The Chinese discovered that if several containers were lined up so that the water flowed from one to another, this arrangement would help overcome the problem of unequal rates of flow. As the next illustration shows, the bottom tank is emptying into a container with a float. The markings on the float indicate the passing of equal intervals of time. Since the bottom tank is continuously being filled by the other tanks, it will always be emptying at the same rate.

CHINESE WATER CLOCK
USING MULTIPLE CONTAINERS

You can test the principle of this apparatus by building your own Chinese water clock.

You will need:
  5 large (2-liter) plastic soda bottles, 4 of them with caps
  hammer
  1 nail
  clock or watch
  ruler
  scissors or knife

Step 1. Cut the bottoms off of four of the bottles. These will have water dripping through them. Cut the top off the fifth bottle. This one will collect the water.

Step 2. Punch a small hole in each of the caps. Put the caps back on the bottles.

Step 3. Fill the four capped bottles with water and stack all five as shown.

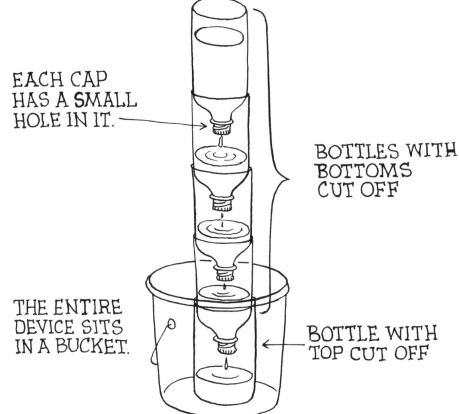

EACH CAP
HAS A SMALL
HOLE IN IT.

BOTTLES WITH
BOTTOMS
CUT OFF

THE ENTIRE
DEVICE SITS
IN A BUCKET.

BOTTLE WITH
TOP CUT OFF

EXPERIMENTS TO TRY

Start timing how long it takes for the water to rise an inch in the bottom water collector.

Does it take the same amount of time for the water to rise the second or third inch?

How could you mark the side of the bottom container to measure minute intervals?

WHAT'S HAPPENING?

As you have already observed, the rate of flow from a single container is not even. In the Chinese clock arrangement, consider what happens in the second container. Water is flowing out, but now some of it is being replaced by water from the first container. However, the rate of flow out is still faster than the rate of flow in, but the change in rate for the second container is not as great as for the first container. The water level in the third container is being replaced at a more even rate than in the second container, but there is still a slight difference in flow out compared to flow in. By adding more containers, the flow in and out can be made equal.

The Egyptian Water Clock

The goal of the Chinese design was to have water flow at a steady rate into the measuring container. Is there a way of constructing a water clock so that the water level in the measuring container rises the same amount in equal intervals of time?

The Egyptian water clock shown in the drawing is one solution to this problem. The Egyptians used a large clay pot similar in shape to the clay pots used today to hold household plants.

EGYPTIAN
WATER
CLOCK

This kind of clock was used as far back as 1500 B.C. Such clocks were mostly used in the court of the kings. One purpose for them was to time speeches in legal cases. Each person arguing in a case had only so many "inches of water" to talk. In military camps these clocks were used to determine how long a soldier stayed on guard before turning the watch over to another.

You have already learned that the rate of the water's flow varies, depending on the shape of the container. Why did the Egyptians choose to make their clock with slanted walls? By making and experimenting with your own model of the Egyptian water clock, you will understand why they did this.

You will need:
> 1 plastic 2-liter soda bottle
> 1 funnel, at least 6 inches across
> 1 medium-size clay or plastic flower pot, about 6 inches high
> 3 ball-point pen tubes
> oil-base modeling clay
> masking tape
> pen or marker

Step 1. Plug up the holes in the soda bottle, funnel, and flower pot with clay.

Step 2. Insert a pen tube through each plug so that the water will be able to drain out.

Step 3. Place a strip of ruled masking tape on the inside of the flower pot and funnel, and on the outside of the soda bottle. These marks should be an inch apart.

Your finished water clocks should look like this:

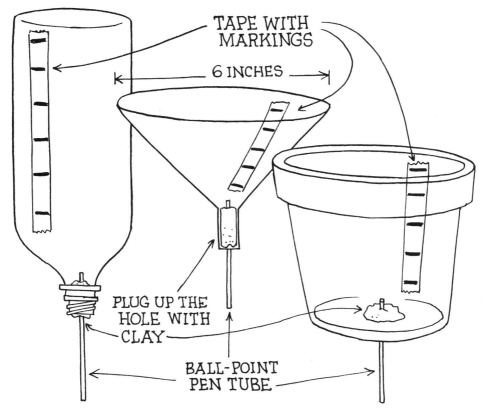

TAPE WITH MARKINGS

6 INCHES

PLUG UP THE HOLE WITH CLAY

BALL-POINT PEN TUBE

EXPERIMENTS TO TRY
Fill the soda bottle with water. Time how long the water takes to move down the first inch. Then time how long it takes to move down the last inch.

Do the same for the funnel and the clay pot. And don't forget to record your results.

WHAT'S HAPPENING?
The results you obtain with the soda bottle should be similar to the ones you got when emptying the milk carton on page 26. The time the water level takes to lower the first inch will be faster than the time it takes to lower the last inch.

The funnel gives a different result. Since the first inch has so much more water than the last inch, it takes much longer for the water level to fall at the top of the container than at the bottom, even though the water is actually draining more slowly when the level reaches the bottom. For this reason the funnel shape still doesn't give equal time intervals.

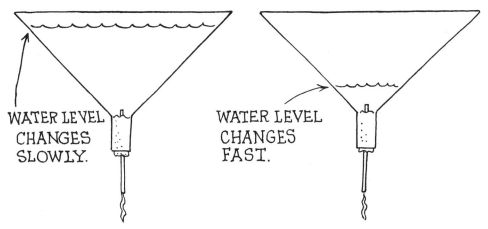

WATER LEVEL
CHANGES
SLOWLY.

WATER LEVEL
CHANGES
FAST.

Water flowing out of the clay pot flows at a more even rate. The first inch of water should lower at close to the same rate as the last inch. Looking at a cross section of a pot will help you understand why this happens.

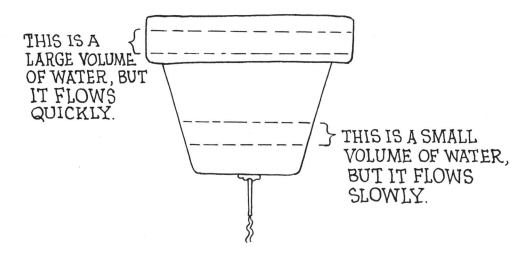

THIS IS A
LARGE VOLUME
OF WATER, BUT
IT FLOWS
QUICKLY.

THIS IS A SMALL
VOLUME OF WATER,
BUT IT FLOWS
SLOWLY.

As you have discovered, water flows faster out of a container when it is filled than when it is nearly empty. Widening the container at the top compensates for the faster flow of water because there will be more water to drain out. By designing the slopes of the sides carefully, you can have the water level fall at a more constant rate. Recent experiments with copies of the Egyptian clay pot found that there was only an error of about ten minutes for each hour mark on the pot.

Sinking Water Clocks

In the Egyptian water clock, water flowed out of a container, and the changing water level was used to indicate intervals of time. Can you think of a way to make a timekeeper that uses the opposite action? Suppose the water flowed through a hole in the bottom of a floating container. Would that solve the problem of varying water pressure?

ARABIC
SINKING
BOWL
CLOCK

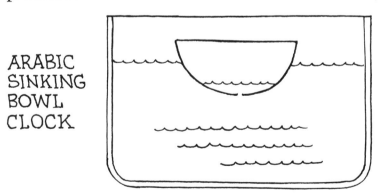

The shape of the Egyptian clay pot was important. Do you think the shape of the sinking bowl matters? Can any kind of container be used? You can find out for yourself.

To make sinking water clocks, you will need some of the containers and materials you gathered on pages 23–24. You might want to use a sink or tub to float your containers in, but a large bucket will do. Here are some questions to think about and try to answer as you experiment. Be sure to have a clock nearby and keep a record of your results.

EXPERIMENTS TO TRY

Does it take a shorter or longer time for a container to sink in water than for water to flow completely out of the same container?

Do tall containers such as milk cartons sink faster than short ones such as margarine tubs or plastic bowls?

Which shapes tip over and which shapes float?

Can you make a clock which measures sixty seconds from the time it is placed in the water until it sinks?

Can you make a clock that measures five minutes or even one hour?

What happens if you add weights such as nails or washers to a container?

Place masking tape on the side of a container. Make a mark every half-inch. Time how long it takes for the water level to rise the first half-inch. Then time the last half-inch. Is there a difference in the rate of flow when the water first starts flowing into the container as compared to when the container is about to sink?

WHAT'S HAPPENING?

One of the first observations you probably made was that most containers tip over easily when placed on the surface of the water. Flat-bottomed ones such as margarine tubs or plastic bowls will sit in the water without any support to keep them from tipping over. This is why the Chinese and Arabs used a flat-bottomed metal bowl.

The flow rate into a container varies from bottom to top. A flat-bottomed margarine tub will fill up faster when it is first placed in the water as compared to when it is almost full. The problem of changing water pressure is encountered here also. The weight of the container helps push water through the hole in the bottom, and initially this happens quickly. As the container fills up, however, the height of the water in the container increases. The column of water inside the container pushes down on the hole. This means the water flowing into the container encounters an increasingly greater force against it at the hole. Therefore, the water flows slower and slower through the hole.

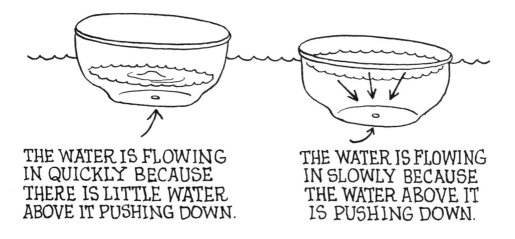

THE WATER IS FLOWING IN QUICKLY BECAUSE THERE IS LITTLE WATER ABOVE IT PUSHING DOWN.

THE WATER IS FLOWING IN SLOWLY BECAUSE THE WATER ABOVE IT IS PUSHING DOWN.

Generally, it takes longer for a container to sink completely in water compared to the same amount of water emptying from that container. The water flowing into a sinking container has to fight against the pressure of the water already there.

Tall containers will sink slower than wide containers such as margarine tubs or plastic bowls, but your results may be inconsistent. Make sure that the holes are the same size and you are comparing equal amounts of water.

The two major factors that determine the sinking rate of the container are the weight of the container and the size of the hole. If you were to compare the rates of a plastic and a metal juice can of the same size, each having the same size hole, you would find that the metal one sinks much faster.

Taking all these observations into consideration, you could make a one-minute clock by choosing the right size container and experimenting with the size of the hole. One way to do this is to try to get a container to sink in slightly more than sixty seconds. Then add a few nails at a time so that the sinking rate gradually speeds up to exactly sixty seconds.

Making a one-hour clock is a bigger challenge. Cut the bottom off a plastic 3-liter soda bottle and make a very small hole in the cap. Put some weights in the neck of the bottle to keep it balanced. Place this water clock in a tub of water and see if you can get it to sink in sixty minutes.

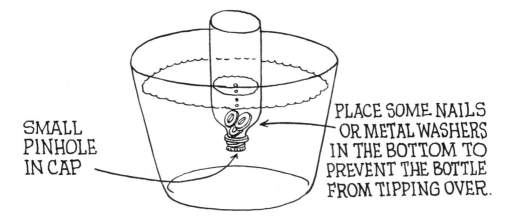

SMALL PINHOLE IN CAP

PLACE SOME NAILS OR METAL WASHERS IN THE BOTTOM TO PREVENT THE BOTTLE FROM TIPPING OVER.

The Siphon Clock

Siphoning water into or out of a container is another possible approach to making a water clock. It would seem that there isn't much difference between water flowing out of a hole in a container and water flowing out of a hole in a piece of tubing. However, if you have ever siphoned water from a tank, you know that the position of the tube is very important in determining how quickly the water will drain. Also, the tubing can be manipulated to control the rate of flow.

Greek inventors were very interested in what could be done with siphons and other water-flow devices. Hero of Alexandria wrote a book containing different kinds of clever devices using the principles of the siphon.

GREEK
SIPHON
CLOCK

Another of his devices showed how to maintain a steady flow of water from one container to another. To understand how this worked, you can try some experiments yourself. Working with siphons is not only fun, but will also help you to understand some of the properties of water pressure.

You will need:

> plastic tubing, 3 feet long by about ¼ inch in
> diameter (You can purchase plastic tubing at
> aquarium supply stores or hardware stores.)
> plastic tubing, 3 feet long by about ½ inch in
> diameter
> buckets or other large containers
> corks
> 1 measuring cup
> rubber bands or string
> clock or watch

There are two ways to start the water moving from one container to another. First, you can place the whole piece of tubing in a bucket of water, letting the water fill the entire length of tubing. Then, placing your fingers over both ends of the tubing, leave one end in the bucket of water and put the other end into a lower container.

Release your finger from the lower end. The water should start flowing.

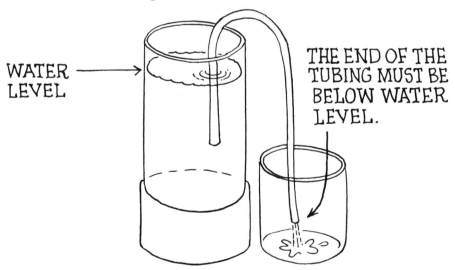

WATER LEVEL →

THE END OF THE TUBING MUST BE BELOW WATER LEVEL.

Another method is to place one end of the tubing in a bucket of water and the other end in a second container and below the level of water in the first. Suck on the lower end of the tubing. This will pull the water through the tubing and start a continuous flow.

Remember that one end must always be kept lower than the water level. Otherwise the water will stop flowing.

EXPERIMENTS TO TRY

Can you get the water to travel back and forth between the containers without stopping and starting the siphon each time?

Using more than one piece of tubing, can you make water travel through several containers?

Can you make the water move faster or slower between the two containers?

Does it make a difference in the flow rate if one end of the tubing is near the water level or far away from it? Time how long it takes to fill up a measuring cup with the water in the container at two or three different levels.

Using string or rubber bands, attach one or more corks to one end of the tubing so that the cork floats in the water. Siphon water from one container to another. Time how long it takes to fill a measuring cup when the cork is near the top of the container and when it is near the bottom. Are the times for each filling the same or different?

Compare the rate of flow of two different diameters of tubing by timing how long it takes to empty a container using each tubing. Remember to keep each end of the tubing in the same positions to make a fair comparison.

WHAT'S HAPPENING?

If two containers are placed side by side, water will flow from one to the other as long as the two water levels are different. As soon as the water levels reach the same height, the flow will stop. The closer the two levels get to each other, the slower the water will flow.

Raising or lowering the end of the tubing through which water is flowing can slow down or speed up the rate. The greater the distance between the end of the tubing and the water level, the faster the flow. Even if you kept both ends in the same position, the rate of flow would still change as the water level in the first container changed. Because the rate of flow is changeable, it seems that siphoning would not be useful for making a water clock.

However, this problem can be overcome by keeping the two ends at the same distance from the water level. You should have discovered this for yourself after you attached the cork to the tubing.

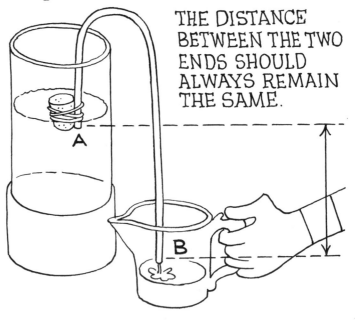

THE DISTANCE BETWEEN THE TWO ENDS SHOULD ALWAYS REMAIN THE SAME.

The end of the tubing at A is always the same height below the water level because it is supported by the floating cork. In addition, as long as you hold the end of the tubing at B the same distance from the level of water in the first container, the rate of flow should remain the same.

You can reverse the direction of the flow by raising the lower container higher than the other container or by raising and lowering the ends of the tubing at A and B, alternately.

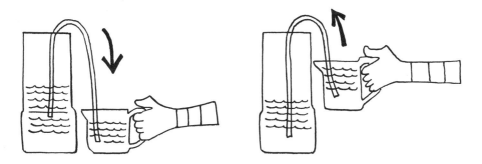

The Floating Valve Clock

Valves are devices which are used to control the flow of liquids. The knobs on your kitchen sink control valves which turn the flow of hot and cold water on and off. Turning the knob one way makes the water flow faster; turning the knob the other way makes it flow slower.

The Greeks invented several kinds of valves that controlled the flow of water. One of them was used to control the flow of water into a water clock. This was one of the first automatic control devices. Once some adjustments were made in the beginning, the flow of water would stay the same despite changing water levels.

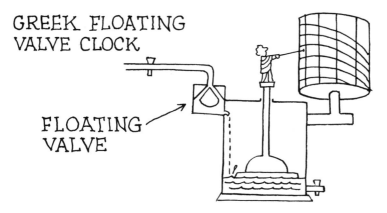

GREEK FLOATING
VALVE CLOCK

FLOATING
VALVE

You can make a model of this Greek device using some simple materials. Some careful adjustment is required, so be patient in trying to get it to work.

You will need:

    1 plastic 1-liter soda bottle
    1 funnel, 2¾ inches at the top (the end must be
        small enough to fit inside the soda bottle)
    2 large buckets or clay pots with plugged-up holes
    1 round balloon
    2 Bic ball-point pens
    oil-base modeling clay
    plastic tubing, 3 feet long by ⅜ inch in diameter
    plastic tubing, 2 feet long by ⅛ inch in diameter
    1 piece of wood, about 3 inches by 3 feet
    1 Styrofoam thread spool (1¼-inch size)
    rubber bands
    ruler
    scissors
    knife
    pliers
    bucket
    clay flower pot

Step 1. Cut the bottom off the soda bottle.

Step 2. With a pair of pliers, pull out the tip and tube holding the ink from one of the pens. Also remove the cap from the other end of the pen. Place the outer ball-point pen tube in the neck of the soda bottle. Plug up the hole with clay to hold the pen in place and prevent any leaks.

Step 3. Attach the ⅜-inch tubing to the end of the pen tube. Put some water inside the bottle to check for leaks. If the pen tube does leak, put clay around the edge where it joins the tubing.

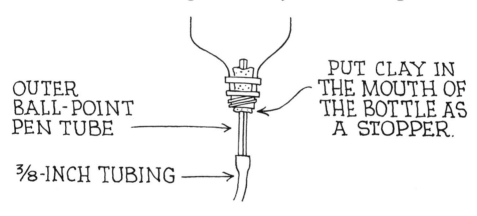

OUTER
BALL-POINT
PEN TUBE ⟶

PUT CLAY IN
THE MOUTH OF
THE BOTTLE AS
A STOPPER.

⅜-INCH TUBING ⟶

Step 4. Attach the bottle to the board with rubber bands.

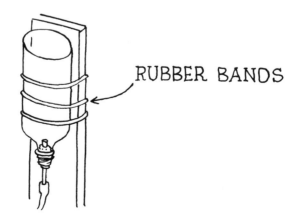

RUBBER BANDS

Step 5. Place the inner tube of the pen inside the neck of the funnel. Plug up the neck with clay to hold the pen tube in place and prevent leaks. Place this in water to test for water-tightness. Add more clay to eliminate any leaks.

Step 6. Cut off the neck of the balloon. Slip the balloon around the wide end of the funnel. Put it in water to make sure the funnel floats and the tube is vertical.

Place this device inside the soda bottle with the balloon side facing down.

A BALLOON IS STRETCHED OVER THE ENTIRE OPENING OF THE FUNNEL.

Step 7. Attach the second outer pen tube to the middle of the ruler with rubber bands.

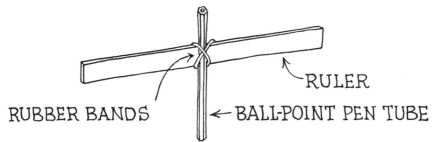

RUBBER BANDS

RULER

← BALL-POINT PEN TUBE

Slide a Styrofoam spool partway onto the untapered end of the pen tube. Cut two 1½-inch-deep slots in opposite sides of the soda bottle so that the ruler will fit snugly into them. Place the ruler device in the bottle with the spool end down.

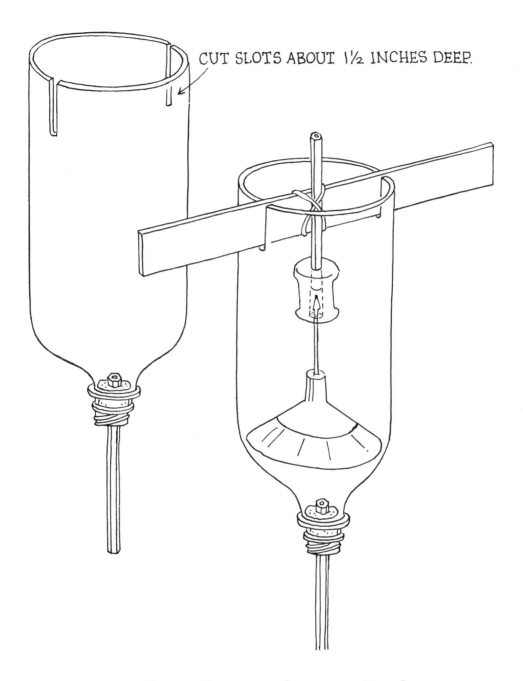

CUT SLOTS ABOUT 1½ INCHES DEEP.

Step 8. Your valve is almost ready to use. But first, some adjustments have to be made.

SETTING UP

Step 1. Attach the end of the ⅛-inch tubing to the other
end of the second ball-point pen tube.

Step 2. Set up the arrangement as shown here.

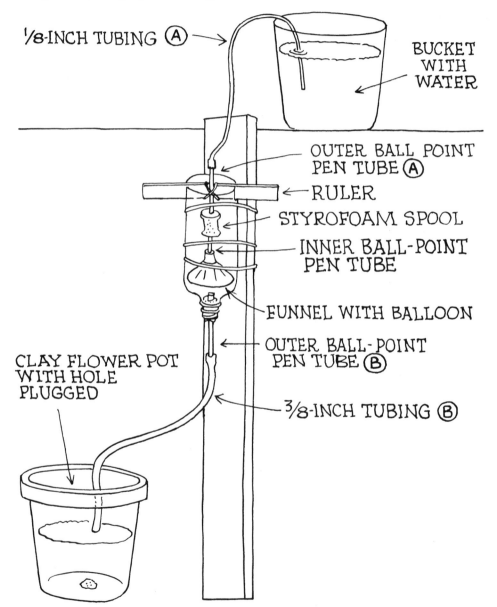

⅛-INCH TUBING Ⓐ →

BUCKET
WITH
WATER

OUTER BALL POINT
PEN TUBE Ⓐ

← RULER

STYROFOAM SPOOL

INNER BALL-POINT
PEN TUBE

FUNNEL WITH BALLOON

OUTER BALL-POINT
PEN TUBE Ⓑ

CLAY FLOWER POT
WITH HOLE
PLUGGED

⅜-INCH TUBING Ⓑ

Water is going to siphon through tubing A, through ball-point pen tube A, down through the inner pen tube in the neck of the bottle, then down around the funnel, ball-point pen tube B, and tubing B, and into the clay pot. The funnel should float as the water enters the soda bottle.

This funnel should also be able to start and stop the flow of water through pen tube A. This action is accomplished by the tip of the inner ball-point pen tube moving up and down inside ball-point pen tube A, and blocking the flow of the water.

You may have to move the inner pen tube up or down, or make other adjustments, to get the floating valve working properly.

Once everything is set up properly, you can start operating the floating valve.

Step 1. Start water moving through tubing A while holding the end of tubing B above the neck of the soda bottle. This will allow water to accumulate in the bottle and cause the funnel to float.

Step 2. When the funnel starts floating, position the tip of the inner pen tube so that it slides inside of the Styrofoam spool on the end of pen tube A.

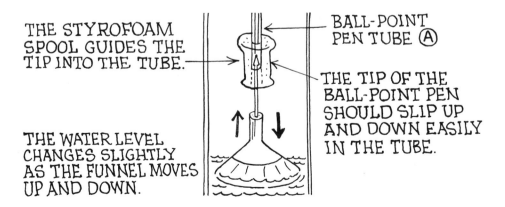

THE STYROFOAM SPOOL GUIDES THE TIP INTO THE TUBE.

BALL-POINT PEN TUBE Ⓐ

THE TIP OF THE BALL-POINT PEN SHOULD SLIP UP AND DOWN EASILY IN THE TUBE.

THE WATER LEVEL CHANGES SLIGHTLY AS THE FUNNEL MOVES UP AND DOWN.

As the water trickles into the bottle, the funnel rises higher and higher, pushing the tip of the pen farther and farther into pen tube A. At some point the pen tip should stop the water from flowing.

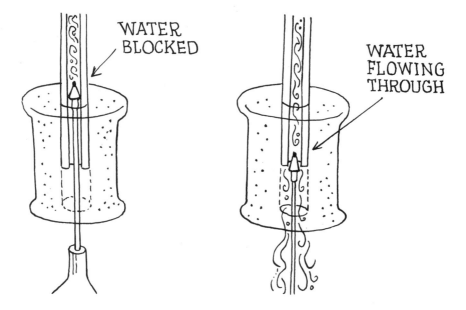

WATER BLOCKED

WATER FLOWING THROUGH

Step 3. Lower the end of tubing B that you have been holding so that water flows into the clay pot. This will lower the water level in the bottle, causing the funnel to move down. As the pen tip slides down in pen tube A, it allows more water to flow into the bottle, replacing the water that flowed out through tubing B.

EXPERIMENTS TO TRY

Raise or lower tubing B to see how the flow rate can be varied.

Can you make a five-minute clock?

Can you make a one-hour clock similar to the Egyptian water clock on page 33?

WHAT'S HAPPENING?

If the water flows out of tubing A at a steady rate, the water will flow into the bottle at a steady rate. Raising or lowering the end of tubing A changes the level of the floating funnel by causing water to flow into the bottle faster or slower. This in turn determines the valve movement, since water is flowing out through tubing B at the same time. Since the water is always flowing at the same rate, this means that the water filling up a cylindrical bottle such as a 2-liter soda bottle will have the water level change in equal time periods for each inch that it rises. Therefore, the height of the water in the bottle can be used to indicate time.

The Water-Wheel Clock

The water clocks you have worked with so far indicate the passing of time using a vertical scale. Most clocks today, however, have circular faces with hands that move around the circle. Back in the eighth century, the Chinese thought of a way to make a water clock that showed the passage of time in a circular manner. The Chinese designed a water-wheel clock.

This water-wheel clock was very large. Historians estimate that it was almost two stories tall. The buckets on the wheel were filled one at a time by water pouring from a storage tank at the top. A lever kept the bucket in place until it reached a certain weight. Then the bucket slipped by the lever, and the next bucket moved into position to be filled. As the wheel slowly turned, it moved a variety of gears and other devices, which in turn moved the hands of the clock.

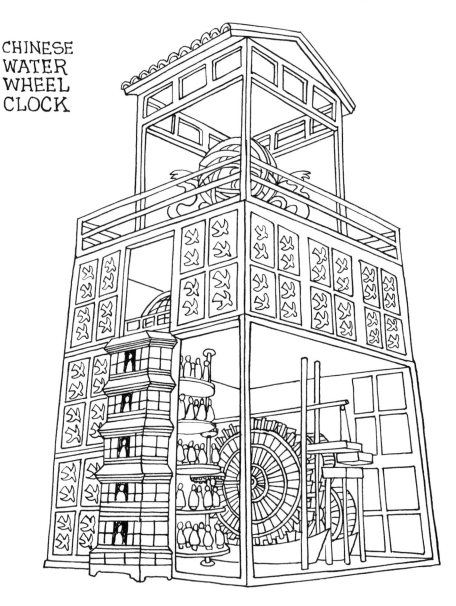

This clock not only indicated the time of day, but also the phases of the moon and the movement of several other heavenly bodies. The clock was located at the court of the emperor and was operated and cared for by a group of scholars. One of their tasks was to advise the farmers

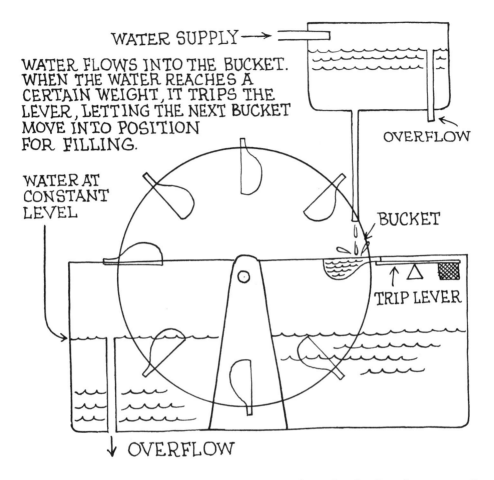

WATER SUPPLY →

WATER FLOWS INTO THE BUCKET. WHEN THE WATER REACHES A CERTAIN WEIGHT, IT TRIPS THE LEVER, LETTING THE NEXT BUCKET MOVE INTO POSITION FOR FILLING.

OVERFLOW

WATER AT CONSTANT LEVEL

BUCKET

TRIP LEVER

↓ OVERFLOW

when to plant their rice. Because the clock also kept track of the seasons, the scholars were able to do this fairly accurately. This clock continued to operate for several centuries, and was one of the most complicated clocks in the ancient world.

If you think about it for a while, you will realize that there are very few water devices that move in a circular manner. There are turbines and lawn sprinklers and water wheels. Each of these moves very quickly. Can you make a model water wheel that moves slowly enough to use as a timekeeping device?

To make the water wheel, you will need:

 2 plastic plates, 8 or 9 inches in diameter
 24 plastic cups (3-ounce size)
 1 ball-point pen tube
 2 Styrofoam thread spools (1¼-inch size)
 masking tape, 1½ inches wide
 1 nail
 scissors
 Note: Since you will be pouring water on your model, plastic plates work best. If you can't get plastic, use three or four heavy paper plates taped together around the edges instead.

Step 1. Punch a hole about ¼ inch in diameter through the center of each of the plates. You can find the center of the plastic plates by finding the point on the plate where it balances on the eraser head of a pencil.

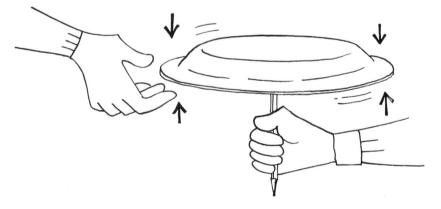

Step 2. Place the two plates back to back. Push the ball-point pen tube through the holes. Then push a Styrofoam spool onto each end of the pen tube against the outside of each plate.

Step 3. Tape the plates together around the inside. (If someone held them while you taped, it would be helpful.)

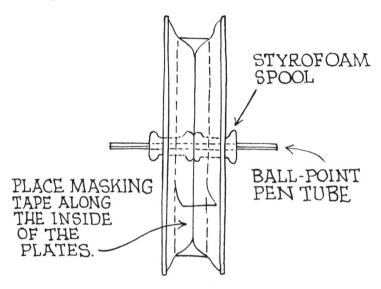

STYROFOAM SPOOL

BALL-POINT PEN TUBE

PLACE MASKING TAPE ALONG THE INSIDE OF THE PLATES.

Step 4. Cut 12 plastic cups in half. Save the part with the rim.

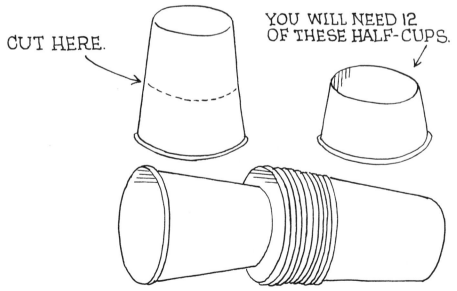

CUT HERE.

YOU WILL NEED 12 OF THESE HALF-CUPS.

Step 5. Tear off a strip of masking tape about 25 inches long. Stick a whole cup to the tape sideways. Then slip the masking tape through the upper section of the cut cup. Slide this half-cup along the tape until it covers the whole cup. This will hold the whole cup securely in place.

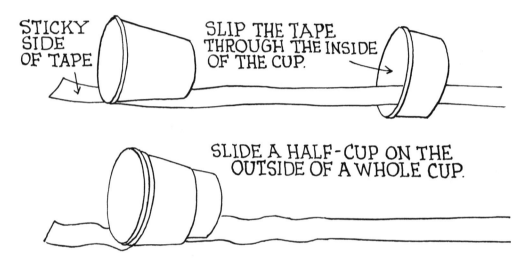

STICKY SIDE OF TAPE

SLIP THE TAPE THROUGH THE INSIDE OF THE CUP.

SLIDE A HALF-CUP ON THE OUTSIDE OF A WHOLE CUP.

Step 6. Repeat this for the other 11 cups. Position them ½ inch from each other.

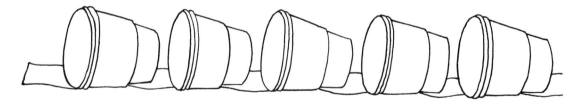

SPACE THE CUPS ½ INCH APART.

Step 7. Wrap this strip of cups around the edge of the plates. Secure it by taping each cup in place.

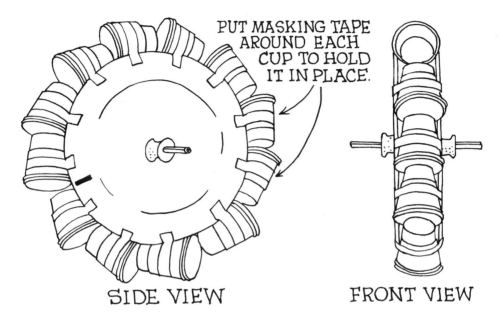

PUT MASKING TAPE AROUND EACH CUP TO HOLD IT IN PLACE.

SIDE VIEW   FRONT VIEW

Step 8. Make a mark on the wheel near the edge of the plate. This mark will help you keep track of the wheel's turning.

SETTING UP

The water wheel should be positioned above a tray. If you make a stand for your model, it will be easier to do the experiments.

To construct a stand, you will need:
> 1 tray (a cat litter tray works well)
> 2 one-pound coffee cans, filled with sand or stones
> 2 sticks, 24 inches long and 1 inch wide, or 2 yardsticks
> 8 to 10 thick rubber bands

1 piece of coat-hanger wire, or any stiff wire, approximately 18 inches long
1 ball-point pen tube
hacksaw
plastic tubing, 3 feet long by about ¼ inch in diameter
bucket

Step 1. Attach a stick vertically to the outside of each coffee can by wrapping 3 or 4 thick rubber bands tightly around the can and stick.

Step 2. Cut a ball-point pen tube in half with a hacksaw. Fasten each half to an upright stick with a rubber band about 12 inches from the top of the can. Make sure the plastic tubes are parallel to the ground.

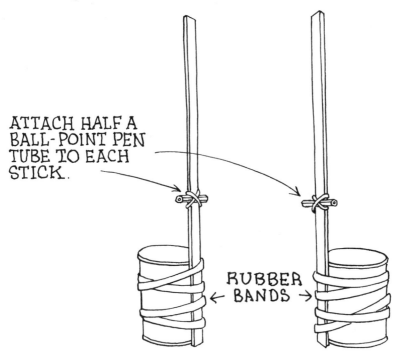

ATTACH HALF A BALL-POINT PEN TUBE TO EACH STICK.

RUBBER
← BANDS →

Step 3. Place a can on each side of the tray. Slide the coat-hanger wire through the pen tube with the cup wheel, then through the pen tubes on the stand. The wheel should be set high enough in the tray so that it doesn't scrape the bottom.

Your set-up should look like this when you are finished:

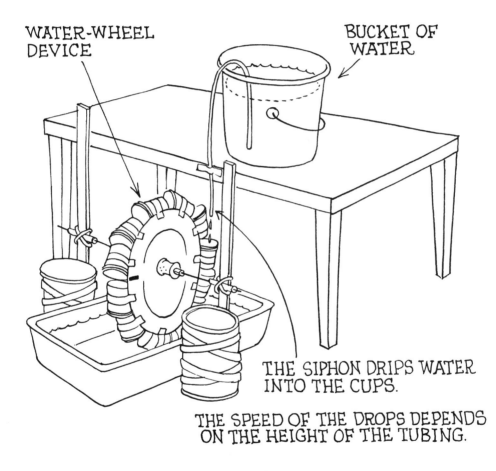

WATER-WHEEL DEVICE

BUCKET OF WATER

THE SIPHON DRIPS WATER INTO THE CUPS.

THE SPEED OF THE DROPS DEPENDS ON THE HEIGHT OF THE TUBING.

Once everything is positioned properly, the wheel should move freely. You can recycle the water by pouring it from the tray back into the bucket.

As you saw in your experiments with the siphons, the rate of water flowing out of the siphon can be controlled by changing the distance of the end of the tubing from the water level in the bucket. The farther away the tubing end is from the water level, the faster the water will flow onto the wheel and the faster the wheel will turn.

Play around with the tubing, moving it up and down, and see how quickly or slowly you can make the wheel move. Try slowing the wheel to one revolution in thirty seconds. If this timing is difficult to achieve, even with the water dripping very slowly, the following method should slow down the wheel even more.

Make sure the bottom of the wheel is close to the bottom of the tray. Pour water into the tray until two or three of the cups are under water.

Now when the water starts dripping into the cups on the top part of the wheel, there will be some resistance to movement. By changing the water level in the tray, you can slow down or speed up the turning of the wheel.

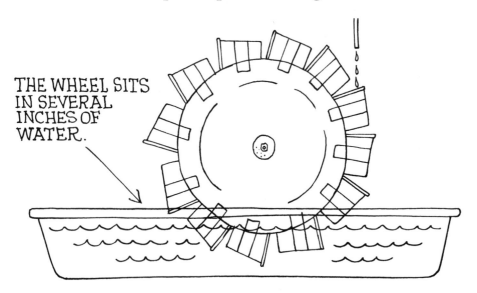

THE WHEEL SITS IN SEVERAL INCHES OF WATER.

EXPERIMENTS TO TRY

Can you now make a clock where the wheel turns once every thirty or sixty seconds?

Try making another wheel with larger plates and larger cups. Can you make a five-minute or even a fifteen-minute clock?

The ultimate challenge is to see if you can make your wheel turn only once in an hour. This means that each of the twelve cups must sit in the same place for about five minutes and the dripping of the water must be very steady. Using the float-valve device (see page 45), larger cups, and a bigger wheel, see how close you can get to making the wheel turn once in an hour.

How quickly can you make one of these wheels move?

The Circular Water Clock

One of the problems of water clocks is that water is constantly being used up. Another problem is that water has to be pumped back into a high tank from a lower one. Can you think of a way to make a water clock that uses the same water over and over again without having to pump it?

A long time ago, the Arabs came up with a design that avoided some of the problems of other water clocks by using the same water over and over again.

The clock consisted of a metal drum that was divided up into chambers. A hanging weight on the axle of the drum forced it to turn. This caused the water to flow from one chamber to another through a tiny hole in the metal plate that separated each chamber. As each chamber in turn

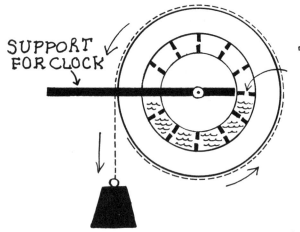

SUPPORT FOR CLOCK

THE WATER MOVES THROUGH THE CHAMBERS AS THE WHEEL TURNS.

filled with water and then emptied, the drum turned.

Clocks like this seem to have originated in Spain during the tenth century. They were frequently found in monasteries. The monks used them to indicate the times of the day and night when they were supposed to pray. These clocks were more reliable and convenient than other water clocks, and they were used in some countries for several hundred years afterward.

To better understand how these clocks worked and to appreciate what an ingenious device they were, you can build your own model.

You will need:
 1 piece of cardboard, 2 feet square
 plastic tubing, 3 feet long by 1¼ inch in diameter
  (The tubing should fit snugly around a ball-point
  pen tube.)
 6 Bic ball-point pens
 2 tuna cans
 1 box of paper clips
 piece of string, approximately 8 feet long

1 plastic coffee-can lid
dishwashing liquid
compass with pencil
1 piece of coat-hanger wire, or any stiff wire,
    approximately 18 inches long
1 T-pin or needle
1 paper half-gallon milk carton
1 drinking straw or eye dropper
knife or scissors
hacksaw
masking tape
pliers
large nail

Step 1. Using the compass and the cardboard, draw and
        cut out a circle that has a radius of 6½ inches.
        Punch a hole in the center of the circle.
Step 2. Punch a hole in the center of the two tuna cans
        with a nail. (To find the center, see page 56 for
        instructions.)
Step 3. Push a ball-point pen tube through the center of
        the two tuna cans. Line up the cans and tape
        them together.

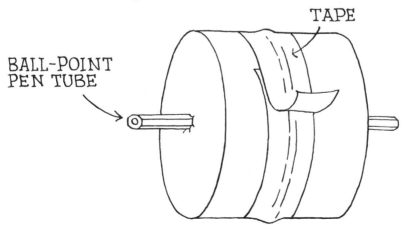

TAPE

BALL-POINT
PEN TUBE

Step 4. Find the center of the plastic coffee-can lid and punch a hole in it. Slide the lid onto the pen tube, positioning it next to one of the tuna cans.

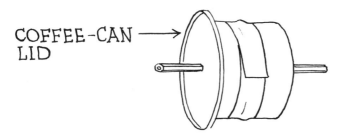

COFFEE-CAN LID

Step 5. Slide the cardboard circle onto the ball-point pen tube next to the other tuna can. Secure the lid to the cans and the cans to the cardboard circle with rubber bands.

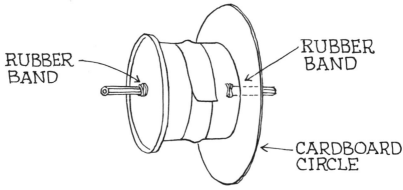

RUBBER BAND

RUBBER BAND

CARDBOARD CIRCLE

Step 6. Using the hacksaw, cut a 1¾-inch piece from the end of a ball-point pen tube. Use the end with the cap, not the pen tip.

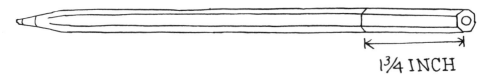

1¾ INCH

Cut 6 tubes in all.

Step 7. Remove the caps from the cut pen tubes. Force the tip of the needle or T-pin through the caps as shown. Use pliers to get a good grip on the T-pin. Make sure you have a clean hole that goes all the way through the plastic. Hold the cap up to the light to check.

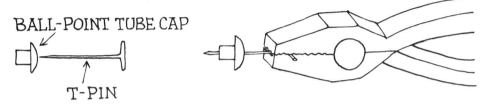

BALL-POINT TUBE CAP

T-PIN

Step 8. Push each cap back into the cut pen-tube pieces.
Step 9. Cut the tubing into six 5¾-inch segments.
Step 10. Join the tubing segments together by inserting the pen-tube pieces into the tubing as connectors.

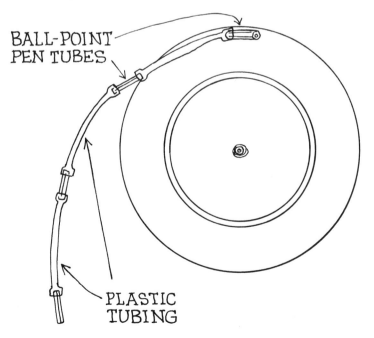

BALL-POINT PEN TUBES

PLASTIC TUBING

Step 11. Tape this ring of tubing near the outer edge of the cardboard circle. Leave one segment open.

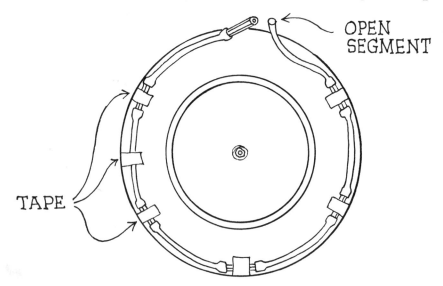

OPEN SEGMENT

TAPE

Step 12. Fill a milk carton with water. Place a few drops of dishwashing liquid in the water and stir.

Step 13. Fill a drinking straw or an eyedropper with the water and drip the water into the open end of the plastic tubing. Add enough water so that at least 6 segments are filled.

Step 14. When you are finished, connect the tubing to make a complete closed circle.

SETTING UP

Set up your clock using the coat-hanger wire to support it between two chairs or from a tall bookshelf.

To make the weight, tape one end of the string on the tuna cans and wrap it around them. Make a hook from a paper clip and tie it to the loose end of the string. Start adding paper clips to the hook, one at a time, until the wheel starts moving. When the right number of paper

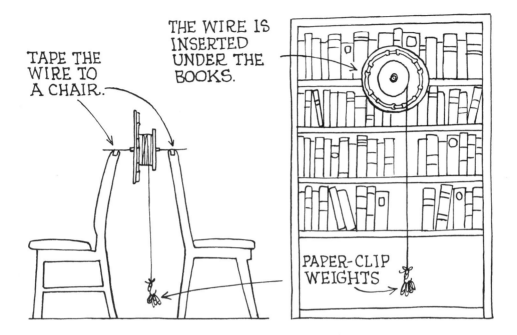

TAPE THE WIRE TO A CHAIR.

THE WIRE IS INSERTED UNDER THE BOOKS.

PAPER-CLIP WEIGHTS

clips has been added, the wheel will move very slowly. If too many clips have been added, the wheel will spin very quickly, causing the paper-clip weight to fall to the floor.

As the wheel moves, watch what happens to the water inside the tubing. If your clock is set up properly, water should move from one piece of tubing to another. After you have observed this action for a while and made any necessary adjustments, you will be ready to try some experiments.

EXPERIMENTS TO TRY

What is the least number of paper clips needed just to keep the wheel moving?

What happens when a few more clips are added above the minimum?

What would happen if there were no water inside the tubing?

What happens if the tubing is almost completely filled
  with water?
What happens if half the tubing is filled with water?
How could you make this arrangement into a one-minute
  or five-minute clock?

WHAT'S HAPPENING?

If you hang weights on the string when there is no water
inside the tubing, the wheel will spin very quickly. With
water filling up six segments, there is a counterbalance to
the weight of the paper clips. While the weight of the
paper clips is forcing the wheel to move in one direction,
the weight of the water in the tubing is resisting this
movement.

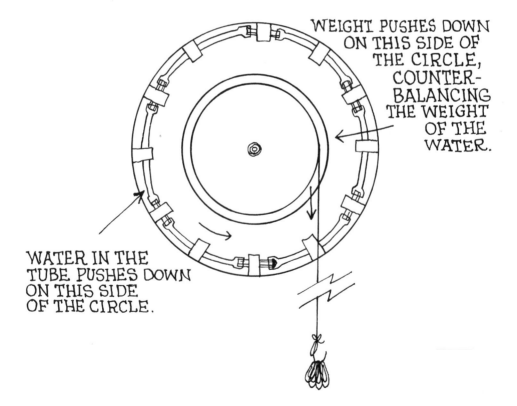

WEIGHT PUSHES DOWN ON THIS SIDE OF THE CIRCLE, COUNTER-BALANCING THE WEIGHT OF THE WATER.

WATER IN THE TUBE PUSHES DOWN ON THIS SIDE OF THE CIRCLE.

Adding just the right amount of water causes the water to be caught on the opposite side of the pulling weight. If all the segments were filled with water, there would be water weight on both sides of the wheel and it wouldn't turn at all. If you kept adding weights to a filled wheel, a point would be reached where the wheel would just spin quickly.

The size of the cap holes also affects the speed of the wheel. Since there are small holes in the caps connecting the tubing, the water flows slowly. The bigger the holes, the more quickly the water would move from one segment to another and the more quickly the wheel would turn.

Soap is added to the water to make it move more easily through the small holes. Water has a tendency to hold itself together as if there were a skin on its surface. It is called *surface tension*. Soap reduces this tendency.

A FURTHER CHALLENGE

If you can find larger, ½-inch- or ¾-inch-diameter tubing at hardware or aquarium supply stores, you can make a longer-running clock. The major change in this device will be the way in which the tubing segments are connected. You will have to wrap masking tape around the end of each ball-point pen tube until it is large enough to fit snugly into the larger-diameter tubing.

Once you have joined all your larger segments together, tape them onto the cardboard circle as before. Fill at least six segments with water and add more paper-clip weights to the string. Now can you make a fifteen-minute clock?

SANDGLASSES

If you lived a long time ago in a part of the world that had very cold winters, you might have awakened one morning to discover that the water in your water clock had frozen solid! How would you have overcome this problem? Would you have thought of using sand?

It is curious that the sandglass did not come into common use until about the fourteenth century. Although sand was already being used as a substitute for water in clocks, and glass had been available for a long time, no one thought to put the two of them together. Eventually, a device was invented that was simply two glass containers connected to each other. Time was measured by how long it took the sand to fall from the top container into the bottom one.

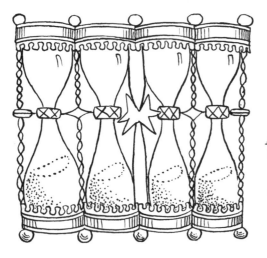

A GERMAN SAND CLOCK FOR TIMES OF 15, 30, 45, AND 60 MINUTES

From the fourteenth century on, this type of timekeeper was very popular. Doctors used a small version to time heartbeats, and astronomers used it to time the movement of the stars. People continued to use sandglasses well into the eighteenth century, despite the fact that accurate mechanical clocks became available.

People still use sandglasses today to time how long to boil an egg. You may even have a device like this in your kitchen.

A Simple Sandglass

Although it is very simple, a sandglass is interesting to observe. The sand falls silently and piles up neatly in the bottom container. You watch and wait, and you never know exactly when the very last grain will fall.

You can make your own sandglasses out of ordinary soda bottles. Once you have made your first model, you can figure out how to construct a three-minute egg timer or an hourglass! Use finely ground, good-quality sand with no larger chunks of foreign matter mixed in. If good-quality sand is not easily available, use salt as a substitute.

You will need:
      10 plastic 1-liter soda bottles, with caps
      5 Styrofoam thread spools, ⅞ inch in diameter
      2 or 3 ball-point pens
      hacksaw
      5 pounds of fine sand or salt
      fine mesh screen

masking tape, 2 inches wide
small nail
funnel
measuring cup
clock or watch

Step 1. Soak the labels off of the bottles. Clean and dry
the bottles thoroughly. This is very important! If
there are even little drops of water left, the sand
or salt will cling together and clog the holes.
Step 2. Sift the sand with a fine mesh screen so that you
have uniform particles.
Step 3. Fill 1 bottle with several inches of sand or salt.
(Using a funnel will make filling the bottle easier.)
Step 4. Connect 2 bottles together in one of the following
ways:
[A] Tape the two bottle caps together as shown.
Punch a small hole with a nail through both caps.
Make sure you get a good, clean hole.

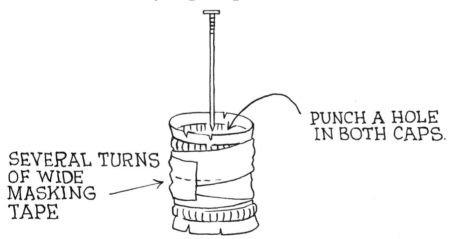

PUNCH A HOLE
IN BOTH CAPS.

SEVERAL TURNS
OF WIDE
MASKING
TAPE

Screw the bottles back into the caps. Be careful
that the tape does not slip off the caps when you
turn the bottles over.

[B] Force a Styrofoam spool halfway into the neck of the bottle with the sand. Then, while holding on to the spool, force the other bottle onto the other half of the spool. (You may need help from another person to do this.) Tape the two necks of the bottles together so they won't separate when you turn them over.

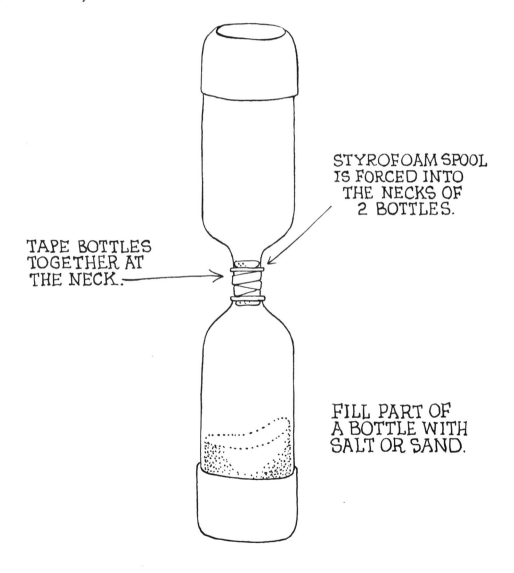

STYROFOAM SPOOL IS FORCED INTO THE NECKS OF 2 BOTTLES.

TAPE BOTTLES TOGETHER AT THE NECK.

FILL PART OF A BOTTLE WITH SALT OR SAND.

SETTING UP

If you want to have a clock that measures a specific time period, you will need to make some adjustments. Start by making a 30-second clock. To do this, time how long it takes for the salt or sand to flow from the top bottle to the bottom one. If this takes more or less than 30 seconds, take the bottles apart and remove or add sand as needed. Reconnect the bottles and time the sand again. Keep doing this until the time of the falling sand is almost exactly 30 seconds. Test your clock several times to make sure it is consistent.

Now you can take up the challenge of making timekeepers of longer duration. Can you make clocks that run for 60 seconds, 120 seconds, or 180 seconds? Each of these times is a multiple of 30 seconds, so you can use your first clock or a measuring cup to figure out the correct amount of sand for your other models.

You can also change the timing of your sandglasses by making smaller size holes. If you are using the Styrofoam spool, you already have a big hole. You can make it smaller by cutting a pen tube down to size with a hacksaw and sliding a piece of it inside this hole.

EXPERIMENTS TO TRY

Use your salt or sand clocks to time different experiments. How long does it take a small ice cube to melt?
How long will a toy top spin?
Fill a 2- or 3-liter bottle. How long does it take to empty completely? Could you make each of these sizes into a one-hour clock?
What different kinds of action of long and short duration can you think of to time?

MECHANICAL CLOCKS

Most clocks today are powered by electricity, whether they are plugged into a small socket or are run by batteries. However, some people still use clocks which operate by a hand-wound spring.

If you look inside one of these clocks, you will find gears of assorted sizes and shapes, a metal spring, and a wheel that rocks back and forth. How do all these parts work together to move the hands on the clock? You'll be able to figure this out by the time you finish this chapter.

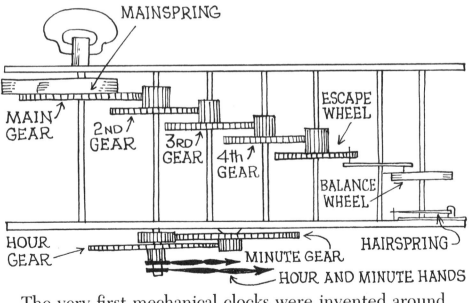

The very first mechanical clocks were invented around the fourteenth century, but just who came up with the original design or where this happened remains a mystery.

These first clocks were mainly one or two gears turning an hour hand. A falling weight hanging on a rope and set in motion by hand at least once a day kept the clock running. A mechanism called the *foliot and verge* rocked back and forth, allowing the weight to fall slowly.

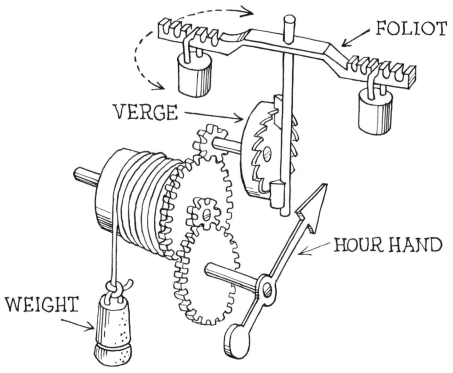

As clock makers continued to experiment and their skill increased, these clocks became more accurate. More gears were added, and many different control mechanisms were invented. Ways were developed to have bells ring each hour. Eventually another hand was added to show the minutes during an hour.

Clock designs became more elaborate and fanciful. Features were added such as a wooden bird popping out of a hole to announce the hour. Cuckoo clocks like these are still in use today.

In some towns in Germany and Italy, very large clock towers were built. A few of these clocks had mechanisms that sent out human figures, some even life size, which would hammer a bell to announce the hours of the day. People continually experimented with mechanical clocks, trying to make them perform all kinds of humanlike actions.

IN THIS GERMAN
AUTOMATON CLOCK
MADE AROUND 1620,
THE FIGURES AT THE
TOP COME OUT
EACH HOUR.

What is curious about all this tinkering is that the clock mechanisms weren't much more accurate or reliable than water clocks. In fact, water clocks continued to be used. But the workings of mechanical clocks fascinated people. These clocks were like scientific toys that challenged people's imagination and ingenuity.

Eventually, important improvements were made that resulted in very accurate timekeepers. But even these useful developments might not have come about if people hadn't explored the playful as well as the practical sides of their mechanical contraptions.

This fascination with mechanical clocks is still with us today. People repair or reconstruct old clocks as a hobby. Artists make sculptures that look like mechanical clocks. It is a real challenge to make even simple models of them. The following pages will show you how to assemble some models for experimenting and help you understand the workings of mechanical clocks.

The Swinging Escapement

Some parts of old clocks are fun to watch in action. For example, the quick movement and sudden stopping of a fifteenth-century German device were particularly humorous. A small weight on a string went flying around one vertical post, unwrapped itself, and then was thrown around another post.

Early clocks were powered by a falling weight. Clock makers had to invent all sorts of devices to ensure that the weight would fall slowly and steadily. A device used for this purpose is called an *escapement*. This control mechanism is one of the most important parts of a clock, since it determines how everything else in the clock moves.

The wrapping escapement is only one kind of control mechanism. Making a model of it, however, will give you a general idea of how a falling weight can be regulated. This model can also be made into a simple clock that runs for a few minutes.

You will need:
> 1 paper half-gallon milk carton
> sand or stones, enough to fill the milk carton
> 3 pieces of coat-hanger wire, or any stiff wire, approximately 10 inches long
> 1 piece of coat-hanger wire, or any stiff wire, approximately 5 inches long
> 1 ball-point pen tube
> 1 Styrofoam thread spool (1¼-inch size)
> 10 washers, ³⁄₁₆ inch in diameter
> string, 6 feet long
> masking tape
> ruler
> 1 paper clip

Step 1. Fill the milk carton with sand or stones. Tape the flap closed. The weight of the sand will help keep the clock from moving around when it is in operation.

Step 2. Bend one end of 2 of the 10-inch-long pieces of wire to make a small loop.

Step 3. Lay the milk carton sideways. Tape the wires to the corners of the milk carton as shown. Make sure they are perfectly straight.

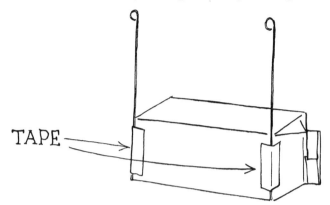

Step 4. Using a ruler, find the midpoint between the two wires. At this point tape the third 10-inch-long piece of wire. Make sure it is perfectly straight. Slide 2 washers onto this middle wire.

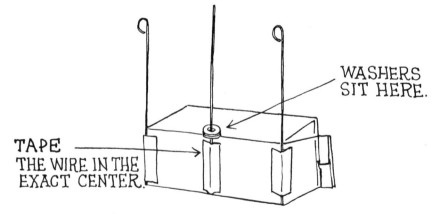

Step 5. Bend the piece of 5-inch-long wire as shown.

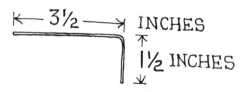

Tape the smaller side of the bent wire to the top of the ball-point pen tube.

Step 6. Tie 3 washers to a piece of string, 7 inches long. Tape the string to the free end of the bent wire. Push a Styrofoam spool onto the bottom of the pen tube.

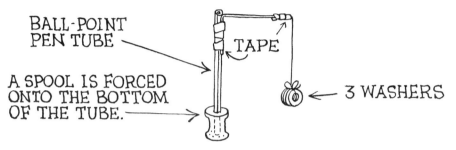

BALL-POINT
PEN TUBE

TAPE

A SPOOL IS FORCED
ONTO THE BOTTOM
OF THE TUBE.

3 WASHERS

Step 7. Tie one end of another piece of string, about 36 inches long, to the spool. Wrap the string around the spool.

Step 8. Make a small hook with a paper clip and tie it to the loose end of the string.

Step 9. Slide the pen tube over the wire in the middle of the milk carton.

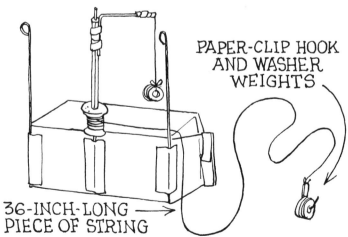

PAPER-CLIP HOOK
AND WASHER
WEIGHTS

36-INCH-LONG
PIECE OF STRING

Your device is almost ready to operate.

SETTING UP

Make a weight for your escapement by slipping several washers onto the end of the paper-clip hook. Let the weight fall to the floor. The falling weight will cause the ball-point pen tube to throw the hanging washers around one of the wires on the end of the milk carton.

The string with the washers will wrap itself around the wire and then unwrap. Then, very quickly, these washers will be thrown around the other wire, wrapping and unwrapping. The cycle will repeat again and again until the weight reaches the floor.

You may have to do some adjusting to get your device working properly. Here are some suggestions for trouble-shooting any problems:

1. If the washers get thrown very quickly from one wire to the other, the string may fly over itself, preventing it from unwrapping. This usually means that the weight is too heavy. Remove a washer and test it again. Continue removing washers until the ball-point pen device works smoothly.
2. The washers may wrap around one wire but not the other. The usual cause of this problem is a bent middle wire. Check to see that the middle wire is straight and perfectly vertical.

EXPERIMENTS TO TRY

Before you begin, time how long it takes for the weight to fall from the milk carton to the floor.

How short can you make the wrapping string that holds the washers and still have your model work? Does changing the length of the string change the amount of time the model will operate?

What happens if you add more washers to the short wrapping string? How does this change the total running time of the model?

Make a pulley arrangement, as shown in the drawing. What does this arrangement do to the running time?

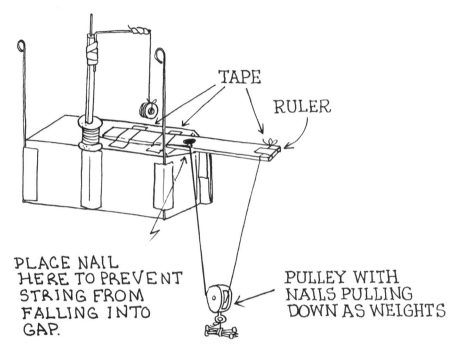

TAPE

RULER

PLACE NAIL HERE TO PREVENT STRING FROM FALLING INTO GAP.

PULLEY WITH NAILS PULLING DOWN AS WEIGHTS

Extend the length of the string holding the weight. Then, put your escapement on a tall bookshelf or ladder. What does this do to the running time?

WHAT'S HAPPENING?

There are several ways of making your "clock" run longer. Increasing the length of the wrapping string results in it taking a longer time for the washers to wrap around each wire. However, if you make it too long, it will tend to become tangled when swinging around the wires. Increasing the number of washers on the wrapping string also helps. If you do this, you will have to also increase the number of nails to make a heavier weight; otherwise the tube with wrapping string won't move. The increased number of washers slows down the wrapping action. Both of the changes may only give you a few more seconds and, in fact, if you don't adjust the weight and length carefully, the total time may be shorter.

The best way to keep your clock running longer is to increase the distance between the model and the floor so that you can attach the weight to the end of a longer piece of string. Putting the model on a ladder, bookcase, or other tall structure is a possible solution. Using the pulley system is another. The pulley arrangement effectively doubles the length of the string.

However, there are limitations to this approach. You can place your clock only so high, and a clock that runs for only a few minutes isn't very useful. The next section shows how clock makers overcame this problem.

The Gears

If you look inside any kind of mechanical clock, you will find many gears. They perform a variety of functions. One set of gears lets the clock run for a long time. To understand how this happens, it is helpful to experiment with some gears.

Some simple and inexpensive wind-up toys operate with gears. You can take one of these apart and examine how it works. Or, you can try making some gears from ordinary materials.

Making gears is a real challenge. They are very precise mechanisms. If only one tooth in a gear is wrong, the whole mechanism will stop working. In this section, you will learn how to make gears of two different sizes from cardboard and drinking straws. They won't work as well as metal gears, but you'll be able to move them well enough to understand how they work in clocks. So be very careful in constructing them, and remember, they are only primitive models.

You will need:
>   1 piece of cardboard, 3 inches long by 10 inches wide
>   1 piece of cardboard, 1 foot square
>   10 plastic drinking straws
>   box of straight pins
>   3 Styrofoam thread spools (1¼-inch size)
>   2 ball-point pen tubes
>   16 nails, 2 inches long
>   compass with pencil
>   knife
>   scissors
>   glue

Step 1. Using the compass and pencil, draw 2 circles 2 inches in diameter from the piece of cardboard. Then draw 2 more circles 5 inches in diameter. Cut them out.

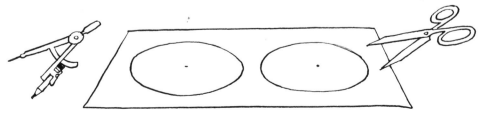

Step 2. Using a copying machine, make 1 copy of the three circles below. Cut out the copied paper circles with scissors.

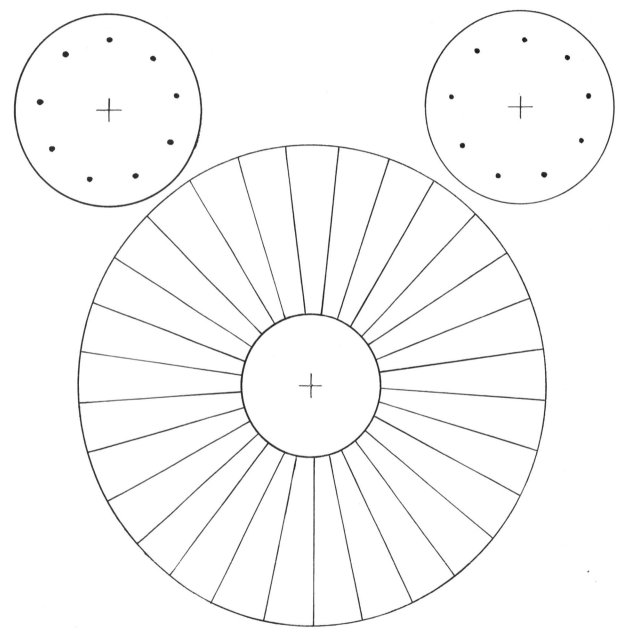

Step 3. Glue the two small, lined paper circles onto the two 2-inch-diameter pieces of cardboard. Line up the two circles, and push nails through both pieces of cardboard as shown.

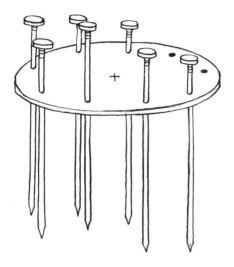 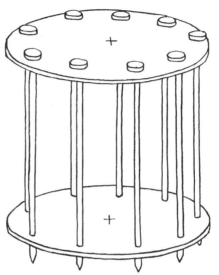

USING THE DOTS AS A GUIDE, INSERT THE NAILS IN A PIECE OF CARDBOARD.

THEN PUSH THE NAILS THROUGH THE DOTS ON THE PAPER GLUED TO THE SECOND PIECE OF CARDBOARD.

Step 4. Separate the two pieces of cardboard, letting the nails remain in one of them. Punch a hole in the center of each piece of cardboard with a pencil or nail. Slide a ball-point pen tube through the center of one of the pieces of cardboard.

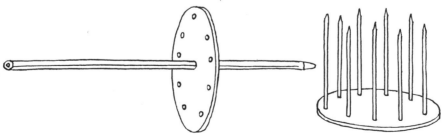

Step 5. Push a Styrofoam spool onto the pen tube. Then slide the other cardboard circle onto the tube, and reconnect the holes and nails.

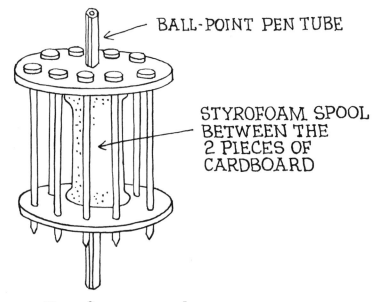

BALL-POINT PEN TUBE

STYROFOAM SPOOL BETWEEN THE 2 PIECES OF CARDBOARD

Your first gear is done.

Step 6. To make the larger gear, glue the larger lined paper circle onto one of the 5-inch-diameter pieces of cardboard. Glue the unlined cardboard circle to the bottom of the lined one.

Step 7. Cut straws into 29 2-inch segments. Cut one end of the straw so that it is pointed as shown.

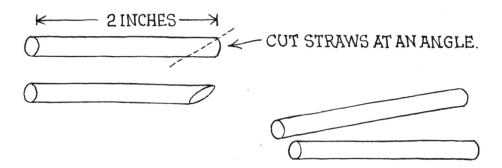

2 INCHES

CUT STRAWS AT AN ANGLE.

Step 8. Line up the straws, one at a time, exactly on top of the lines shown on the paper. The pointed end sticks out from the edge of the cardboard. Fasten each straw in place with 2 pins. The pins should stick out a little from the top, but should penetrate both pieces of cardboard. Keep adding straws until all the lines have been covered. (The position of the straws and the distance they stick out from the cardboard are very important, so take your time.)

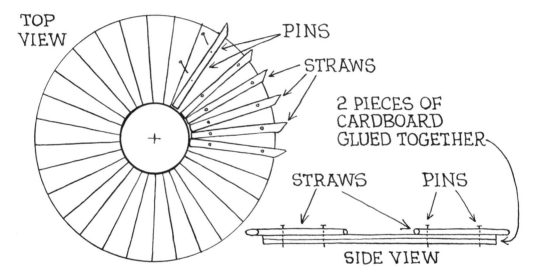

Step 9. Punch a hole in the middle of the cardboard wheel with a pencil or nail. Slide a ball-point pen through this hole. Place a Styrofoam spool on each side of the cardboard wheel.

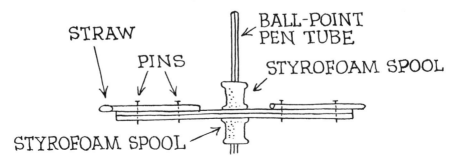

SETTING UP

At first just test the gears by watching how they move in relation to each other. Push one of the nails through the 1-foot piece of cardboard so that the nail sticks up vertically on one side. Slide the larger gear onto this nail. Line up the smaller gear so that it sits next to the larger one. The straws should just about sit in between the nails. Push another nail through the cardboard to hold this gear in place.

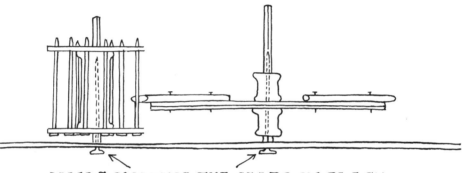

NAILS HOLDING THE GEARS IN PLACE

Turn each gear a few times to see how well they mesh together. If they are too close together, they may jam. Move the gears farther apart until they work together easily.

EXPERIMENTS TO TRY

Make a mark on both gears at one point where they meet.
    Slowly turn the big gear and watch what happens to the smaller gear. How many times does the mark on the smaller gear move around before it again meets the mark on the bigger gear?
Start over again and see how many times you have to move the small gear to make the big gear move once.

WHAT'S HAPPENING?

The 5-inch gear is two-and-a-half times as big as the 2-inch one. If you turn the big gear one revolution, the small gear should make two-and-a-half revolutions. If you turn the small gear one revolution, the big one should only make half a turn.

This observation about the rate at which gears revolve in relation to their size is a simple one, but it is very important in understanding why gears are used in clocks. Remember your experiments with the wrapping escapement? The device did not continue to operate for a long time because the weight quickly reached the floor. Suppose, however, that the pen tube holding the swinging string is attached to gear A, which is turned by a larger gear B. Gear B is connected to the string with the falling weight that moves the entire mechanism.

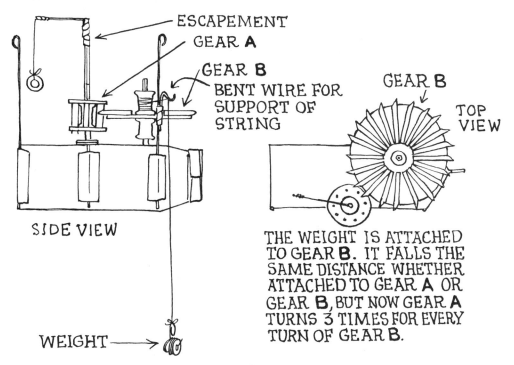

ESCAPEMENT
GEAR **A**
GEAR **B**
BENT WIRE FOR
SUPPORT OF
STRING

GEAR **B**
TOP
VIEW

SIDE VIEW

WEIGHT →

THE WEIGHT IS ATTACHED
TO GEAR **B**. IT FALLS THE
SAME DISTANCE WHETHER
ATTACHED TO GEAR **A** OR
GEAR **B**, BUT NOW GEAR **A**
TURNS 3 TIMES FOR EVERY
TURN OF GEAR **B**.

When the string is attached to gear B, it still falls the same distance as before. However, now it is moving a gear that we know will make one revolution for every two revolutions of the gear that moves the swinging washers. This means that the weight falls through the same distance but causes the washers to make twice as many swings as before. This is a way of making a longer-running clock. In a real mechanical clock, the swinging mechanism or escapement would be driven by a set of gears to extend the running time of the clock.

Imagine if there were even more gears attached, each one bigger than the other. The operating time of the clock would be increased in proportion to the number of gears and the ratio of their sizes to each other. (As you add more gears, however, the power needed to operate the system increases. More weight would have to be added to the string to make the gears move.)

In fact, most mechanical clocks do have several gears between the source of power and the escapement. Their alignment usually looks like this:

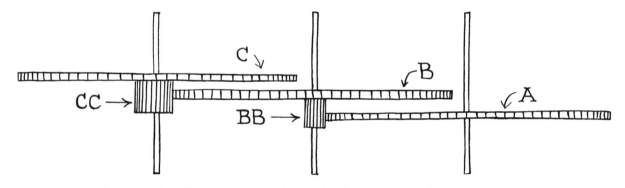

The teeth of gear A mesh with the teeth of gear BB. Gear BB and gear B are attached to each other. The teeth of gear B mesh with those of gear CC, and gear CC is attached to C. If gear BB turns ten times to every one turn of gear A, gear B also turns ten times. But gear B also turns gear CC. If gear CC turns ten times every time gear B turns once, this means that gear A only has to turn one revolution to make gear C turn a hundred times! You can see how useful gears are in clock making!

The Pendulum Escapement

This escapement combines the turning of a gear with the rocking of a pendulum. On real clocks this mechanism runs quite smoothly. The back-and-forth motion of the model you will be making will probably be a bit irregular, but it is still fun to watch. Experimenting with the model will help you understand how escapements work in today's clocks and watches.

The pendulum escapement was invented in part by Galileo and in part by a Dutch mathematician named Huygens. Galileo described this escapement in writing, but never managed to build one. Huygens improved on Galileo's idea by making some careful mathematical calculations. Huygens also engaged a clock maker to build this escapement and thereby demonstrated that the idea was a practical one. The pendulum escapement was a very important advancement in clock making because it was the first one that could precisely control the falling weight.

The movement of a pendulum can be very carefully controlled. By making the pendulum arm a precise length and keeping its swing within certain limits, its back-and-forth motion will always be the same. For a long time many large, standing clocks used this kind of escapement. If you see a grandfather clock today, you can watch the pendulum swing.

TICK! TOCK! TICK! TOCK!

A pendulum escapement is a very challenging model to build, but once you get it working, you'll find it was worth the effort.

You will need:

      2 plastic plates, 8 inches in diameter

      15 plastic cups, 3-ounce size

      2 ball-point pen tubes

      3 Styrofoam thread spools (1¼-inch size)

      1 piece of wood, approximately 21 inches long, or
        a yardstick

      2 pieces of coat-hanger wire, or any sturdy wire,
        14 inches long

      piece of string, 3 feet long

      masking tape

      4 rubber bands

      nails

Step 1. Punch a hole with a nail through the center of each of the plastic plates. (See page 56.) Place the plates back to back and slide a ball-point pen tube through the holes.

Step 2. Push a Styrofoam spool onto the pen tube on each side of the plates to hold them securely. Place a third spool at one end of the pen tube.

PLACE TAPE IN THE GAP BETWEEN THE 2 PLATES.

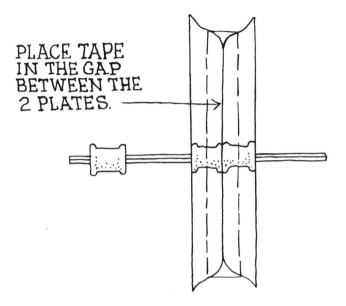

Step 3. Place masking tape between the plates, as shown.
Step 4. Line up 13 cups along the edge of a table or against a long stick to keep them straight. Join the cups together with tape, being careful to keep the cups in a straight line. There should be no gaps between the cups.

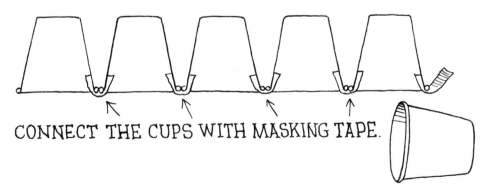

CONNECT THE CUPS WITH MASKING TAPE.

Step 5. Carefully lift the row of joined cups and place it over the edge of the plastic plates.

Close this row of cups by stretching the two end cups and sliding one end cup over the other.

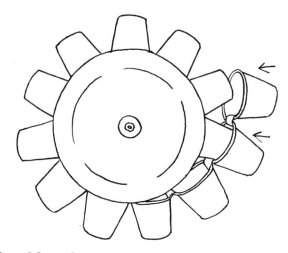

This should make a complete circle, fitting very snugly on the perimeter of the plates.

Step 6. Make sure all the cups are sitting on the edges of the two plates. Place pieces of tape between the cups to secure them to the plates.

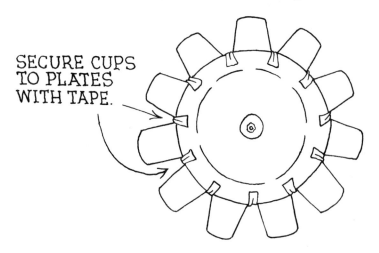

SECURE CUPS TO PLATES WITH TAPE.

Step 7. Tie one end of a piece of string 36 inches long to the Styrofoam spool on the end of the ball-point pen tube. You have just made the gear section of the pendulum escapement.

Step 8. To make the pendulum, cut 2 cups in half as shown.

CUT THE CUP IN HALF, UP THE SIDE AND ALONG THE BOTTOM EDGE.

Step 9. Attach these 2 cups to the piece of wood with rubber bands. Also use a rubber band to attach a ball-point pen tube between the two cups.

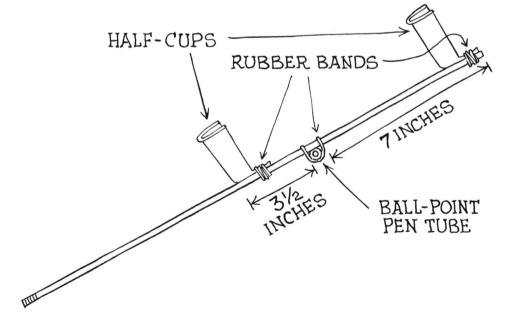

HALF-CUPS

RUBBER BANDS

7 INCHES

3½ INCHES

BALL-POINT PEN TUBE

SETTING UP

Step 1. Place the gear between two tables or chairs, using the 14-inch piece of wire to support it. Tape the wire in place.

Step 2. Place the pendulum between the chairs or tables using the second 14-inch piece of wire. Position it so that the two half-cups of the pendulum mesh with the gear cups. The position of the cups on the stick in relation to the cups on the gear is very important. Line up the cups very carefully as shown. The bottom half-cup should be slightly below a cup on the gear.

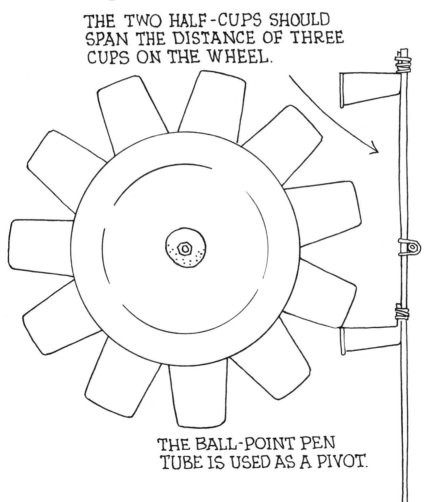

THE TWO HALF-CUPS SHOULD SPAN THE DISTANCE OF THREE CUPS ON THE WHEEL.

THE BALL-POINT PEN TUBE IS USED AS A PIVOT.

Step 3. Tape a few nails on the bottom of the stick to make it hang vertically.

Step 4. Join about three nails together with a rubber band and attach them to the end of the string as a weight. Wind up the string onto the spool.

Here is how your pendulum escapement should work. As the falling weight forces the gear to move, the bottom half-cup on the pendulum is pushed away. This causes the bottom part of the stick to move away from the gear while the top part moves toward the gear. The half-cup on the top part of the pendulum moves toward the wheel, stopping the movement of the gear very briefly. The gear

HERE IS
HOW THE
PENDULUM
ESCAPEMENT
SHOULD
WORK:

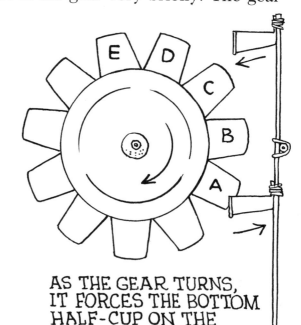

AS THE GEAR TURNS,
IT FORCES THE BOTTOM
HALF-CUP ON THE
STICK TO MOVE.

is still being forced to move by the falling weight, so the cup on the gear pushes against the top half-cup on the pendulum and pushes it away.

The stick has changed position resulting in the bottom half-cup moving into position to stop the gears again. The whole sequence of starting and stopping repeats itself until the weight hits the floor.

This kind of starting-and-stopping motion occurs in many different kinds of escapements. There may be different-shaped teeth on the gear or a device other than a pendulum, but all these various escapements produce a rhythmic motion that makes the *tick-tock* sound you hear in clocks.

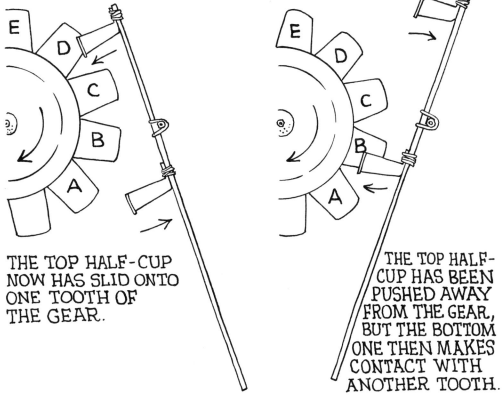

THE TOP HALF-CUP NOW HAS SLID ONTO ONE TOOTH OF THE GEAR.

THE TOP HALF-CUP HAS BEEN PUSHED AWAY FROM THE GEAR, BUT THE BOTTOM ONE THEN MAKES CONTACT WITH ANOTHER TOOTH.

HOW MECHANICAL CLOCKS WORK

So far you have only experimented with a few parts of a mechanical clock. A real clock is full of gears, the escapement, dials, and other moving parts. The best way to understand how all these parts work together to tell time is to look inside a real clock.

Most clocks today are electrically driven. However, there is still one kind of clock available that is similar to traditional mechanical clocks. This is the alarm clock that people use to wake themselves up in the morning.

You can buy one in a department store or try to find one secondhand at a garage sale or junk shop.

Look inside an alarm clock and try to figure out what is going on. Remember, it is usually much easier to take something apart than to put it back together, so before going too far with your pliers and screwdriver, examine the contents of your clock carefully.

First you should remove the back and, if possible, the front covers of the clock with a screwdriver. The wind-up keys can usually be unscrewed by twisting them in the opposite direction of the winding action. (Keep the screws, keys, and other parts in a box, so you won't lose them.)

Spend some time watching the movement of the gears and the *escapement*, which is a circular wheel attached to a very fine spring, called the *balance spring*.

Compare your clock to the one in the drawing. What looks the same? What is different?

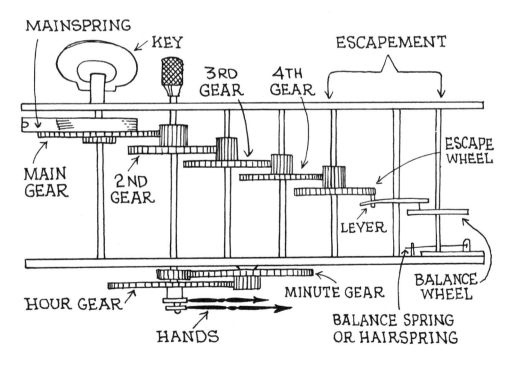

MAINSPRING

KEY

3RD GEAR

4TH GEAR

ESCAPEMENT

MAIN GEAR

2ND GEAR

ESCAPE WHEEL

LEVER

HOUR GEAR

MINUTE GEAR

BALANCE WHEEL

HANDS

BALANCE SPRING OR HAIRSPRING

Most mechanical clocks can be divided into five sections. These are the power source, the gear train, the escapement, the gear that turns the hands, and the alarm mechanism. Here is how each of these works.

The Power Source

Your models of the wrapping escapement and pendulum were both powered by a falling weight on a string. In an alarm clock the source of power is a metal spring, called the *mainspring*. This piece of metal may seem small, but when twisted in a compact spiral, it can exert a surprising amount of force. As you turn the key on the back of the clock, it twists the mainspring into a tight spiral. This spiral of metal is above the main gear, and as it unwinds, it in turn moves a set of gears—the second, third, and fourth gear in the illustration. Some clocks have two metal springs. The smaller one powers the mechanism that rings the alarm.

The use of the metal spring as a power source was introduced around 1500 by a German clock maker. It was a very important invention because it allowed clock makers to design much smaller clocks, eventually resulting in the pocket watch.

The Gear Train

In experimenting with your model gears, you discovered that they can extend the operating time of a clock. The more gears that are connected to each other, the longer the operating time.

Carefully examine the gears inside your alarm clock. Start with the gear that is attached to the mainspring, called the *main gear*. It will be turning a much smaller gear, which is called a *pinion gear*. On the same shaft as the pinion gear is another gear, called the second gear in the illustration. This arrangement may repeat itself several times before it ends up turning a small wheel that rotates back and forth very quickly. Between the spring and this rotating or swinging wheel, called the *balance wheel*, there are usually three or four axles with a big gear and small cylindrical gear. These are the second, third, and fourth gears in the illustration. This particular lineup is called a *gear train*. If your clock didn't have all these gears, you would have to wind it every few hours instead of every day or so.

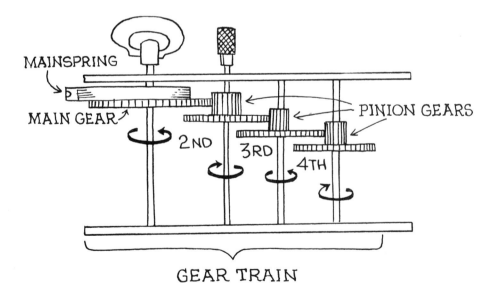

As you watch these gears, it may seem as if the bigger ones (second, third gears) near the mainspring are not moving at all. In fact, they are moving, but very slowly.

To see this happening, make a mark with a pencil or felt-tip pen on each of the gears. Line up the marks on two of the gears. Watch what happens to these marks. On the gear near the balance wheel (fourth gear), the change in position will be noticeable in a few minutes. The gears near the mainspring (second and third gears) move much more slowly. Let the clock run for more than half an hour and check them again. Have the marks on the gears made one full revolution? While you wait for this to happen, spend more time watching the swinging balance wheel.

The Escapement

At the end of the gear train that starts at the mainspring and leads up to the swinging or balance wheel, there is one gear that doesn't have regular teeth. Its teeth look more like hooks. This is the fastest-moving gear, and it is called the *escape wheel*.

Next to the escape wheel is a very small arm or lever that lets the "hooks" slip by at a regular rate. The "hooks" of the escape wheel are similar to the cups of your model gear wheel. The pins that are on the end of the lever are similar to the half-cups of your model pendulum. Remember how your pendulum escapement model worked? As the falling weight turned the gear wheel, it forced the half-cups on the pendulum stick to move, causing the stick to swing back and forth. This action is similar to that of the small *lever* moving back and forth with the escape wheel.

There is one big difference here. The weight of your vertical pendulum model caused it to fall back to a vertical position each time the cup on the moving gear wheel

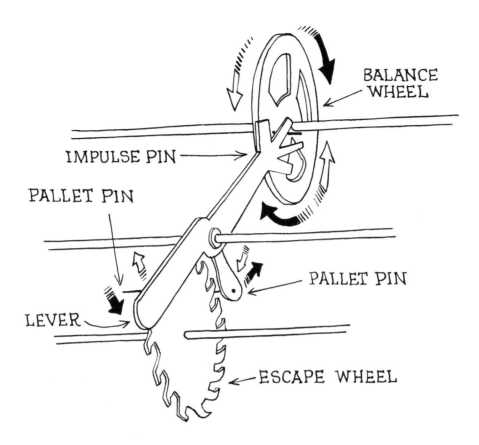

IMPULSE PIN

PALLET PIN

BALANCE WHEEL

PALLET PIN

LEVER

ESCAPE WHEEL

pushed on it. In modern mechanical clocks, a very fine spring called the *hairspring*, attached to the balance wheel, performs the same kind of function. Here's how it happens:

On the small lever there are two *pallet pins*. These are like the two half-cups on your vertical pendulum model. They are pushed back and forth by the escape wheel.

On the other end of the lever, there is a slotlike arrangement. When the lever is moved by the escape wheel, the slotted end pushes against an *impulse pin* on the balance wheel. This causes the balance wheel to start moving, expanding or contracting the hairspring until the resistance of the hairspring pushes the balance wheel back in the opposite direction. As the balance wheel comes back, the impulse pin hits up against the other side of the slot. In the meantime, the lever arm has received another push from the escape wheel, and this in turn pushes the impulse pin the other way.

All this back-and-forth motion happens very quickly. To help you see what is happening, put your finger on the escape wheel and stop it. Then move this gear gently and slowly. You can start and stop the motion, and see how the different parts mesh with each other.

The Hands

On the back of the clock is one knob that turns both the minute and hour hands on the face of the clock. Follow the axle of this knob to the front of the clock. You will see that this end of the axle is attached to a group of gears. One gear—the *minute wheel*—is responsible for moving the minute hand completely around the face of the clock once an hour. Another gear—the *hour wheel*—is responsible for moving the hour hand around the face of the clock once every twelve hours. This gear arrangement is designed so that for every one revolution of the minute wheel there is one-twelfth of a revolution of the hour wheel.

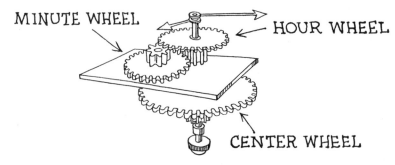

MINUTE WHEEL   HOUR WHEEL

CENTER WHEEL

The Alarm Mechanism

You can set an alarm clock so that it will ring at a very specific time. Mechanisms vary, but there are several features that most alarm clocks have in common. Look inside your clock to see what particular arrangements you have. A knob usually connects directly to a colored alarm hand on the face of the clock and turns this hand to the time you want the alarm to go off.

Most clocks have a separate metal spring which powers the mechanism that rings the alarm. This spring must be wound up if the alarm is to ring. There is a button on the outside of the clock which turns the alarm mechanism on and off. To see how this works, follow each of the steps in the sequence of action: Wind up the metal spring, pull the knob out so the alarm will ring, and turn the knob that selects the time for the alarm to go off. Do this several times, watching how the gears inside turn just before the alarm goes off. What makes the bell ring?

The alarm mechanism in this kind of clock is simple compared to ones made hundreds of years ago. Some clocks were designed to ring every fifteen minutes. Others would chime or play a melody every hour on the hour. More elaborate ones kept track of the phases of the moon and the cycles of some planets. All of these extra arrangements required more gears and more mechanical devices. They didn't make the clock any more accurate, but people enjoyed the challenge of inventing such elaborate mechanisms.

BECOME A CLOCKMAKER

People throughout the ages have invented many different ways of measuring time. The models presented in this book represent only a sampling of some of the most important of these ways.

Even today, scientists, engineers, and artists have not reached the end of their timekeeping explorations. Some are still working with material and devices used a long time ago. In a shopping center in Paris, for instance, there stands a two-story water clock. Water keeps a huge pendulum moving back and forth, and the rising and falling water levels in glass tubes indicate the time of day. Others are experimenting in the laboratories with very special materials and equipment. Recently, scientists made an atomic clock which measures time down to a billionth of a second.

Now that you, too, have built models of clocks and experimented with them, you have the know-how to explore and make discoveries on your own. Why not try inventing your own kind of clock? It may be simple or complicated, but even if your model doesn't keep perfect time, you will still have had the fun of becoming a clockmaker.

681.113 Zubrowski, Bernie.
ZUB
        Clocks

    $12.88   18ろ1

DATE			